# A YEAR INSIDE MS-13

# A YEAR
# INSIDE MS-13

## See, Hear, and Shut Up

**Juan José Martínez d'Aubuisson**

Translated from the Spanish
by Natascha Uhlmann

O/R

OR Books

New York · London

All rights information: rights@orbooks.com
Visit our website at www.orbooks.com

First printing 2019

Cataloging-in-Publication data is available from the Library of Congress.
A catalog record for this book is available from the British Library.

Typeset by Lapiz Digital.

Published by OR Books for the book trade in partnership with Counterpoint Press.

paperback ISBN 978-1-949017-15-1 • ebook ISBN 978-1-949017-16-8

# Contents

# Prologue: Juan's Madness

## Óscar Martínez[1]

J UAN HAD AN old motorcycle. It was an inexpensive model, without gears even, some cheap Chinese brand that no enthusiast would recognize. Juan called her Samantha. Several times a week, Juan and Samantha had to traverse several neighborhoods dominated by the rival gang, Barrio 18, in order to get to Juan's research site in the last neighborhood on the hill: the Buenos Aires neighborhood in San Salvador, MS territory. El Salvador is a country with more dividing lines than you'd find on a map. The unmapped lines, the ones delineating rival gangs, are, if anything, more real than those found on maps.

One night in 2010, Juan was returning from the Buenos Aires neighborhood, Samantha's feeble motor straining. He had spent the day conducting an ethnographic study of Guanacos Criminales Salvatrucha, an MS-13 *clica*.[2] Samantha, now in Barrio 18 territory,

---

1  Author of *The Beast: Riding the Rails and Dodging Narcos on the Migrant Trail* and *A History of Violence: Living and Dying in Central America*.

2  A clica, or clique or cell, is the smallest unit of a gang. In this sense, Mara Salvatrucha (MS-13) is what we call the amalgamation of clicas that consider

sputtered to a halt. It was night, he was a young man on a motorcycle; he was a young man, tattooed and long haired on a motorcycle; he was a young man, tattooed and long haired and on a motorcycle *that had just stopped in enemy territory*. Juan told me one night over a drink that he knew this could end very badly. He weighed his options: call the cops, continue on foot, seek help at a stranger's door . . . and picked the best one: *beg* Samantha to move. He asked his cheap Chinese motorcycle to please move. He promised her a full tune-up if she got him out of Barrio 18's hood. And just as the shadows crept up, with a kick of the lever Samantha sputtered alive, and begrudgingly took them to safety. Sometimes it is necessary to be a little mad in order to conduct the sort of work Juan discusses in this book. It is necessary to set aside logic and rationality and beg a motorcycle to come back to life.

Juan is an anthropologist. Juan is an anthropologist dedicated to studying gangs, primarily Mara Salvatrucha, but he's also had encounters with Barrio 18 and the legion of deportees from the US who, while there, joined one of the dozens of Latino gangs from Southern California who refer to themselves as Sureños (Southerners). Juan has interviewed founders of MS, leaders of MS, retirees, and pawns; also traitors to MS, victims of MS, and the officials who want them dead.

Juan is also my brother. That said, and I say this without hesitation: Juan is the academic who best understands the most dangerous gang in the world, the MS. He best understands them because as an academic—a word which each day commands less respect—he's renounced the comfort of lecture halls and air conditioners; he's

---

themselves parts of the gang. The majority of these use names that end in LS (Locos Salvatrucha) to differentiate themselves from those in Barrio 18.

renounced the writing of abstract tracts accessible only to those with advanced degrees. As an academic, Juan has renounced the classist norms of academia that dictate whose stories are worthy of being told.

The greatest testament to Juan's unorthodox style is this book. This book does not set out to be academic. However, it elucidates how a strange academic who talks to motorcycles made sense of— makes sense of—the most violent corner of the planet. When Juan played cops and robbers with neighborhood kids, he knew he was *working*. When Juan spent long evenings watching Destino, one of the clica's leaders, make bread, he knew he was *researching*. When Juan scrawled notes on how the gang coerced a town drunkard to buy them cigarettes, Juan knew this was his *job*. He knew it, too, when he was the only non-gang member present at their gatherings, and when Destino told him his inner secrets and when Little Down started to take control and Juan saw it all, due to his patience, due to his understanding that *remaining* is key. Each day he'd arrive home with Samantha and a journal full of notes.

Sometimes, at family dinners or nights at the bar, you could tell that *remaining* was taking its own toll on him. Juan would speak like a gang member in flashes, as if it took him a few moments to distance himself from that which he'd jotted in his journal.

What you are about to read are the field notes of a mad anthropologist who made the journey again and again to understand what it meant, as a community, to live with Mara Salvatrucha. Juan decided that the gang, for his readers, should cease to be two glaring initials and instead take on a new meaning, informed by names, dynamics, words, children, the dead, their homes . . .

Reading an academic who is allergic to air-conditioned lecture halls is a gift. Reading him on Mara Salvatrucha is doubly so. There exist few criminal groups about whom so many stupid things have been published. From the pretentious—a piece that sought to link the Maras and the Zetas—to the ignorant—the editorial that tried to illustrate, with pictures of rock stars downloaded from the internet, the symbology of gang tattoos. There are (aren't there always) pizzeria journalists who prepare and deliver articles in thirty minutes or less, that tell us of gangs, their satanic rituals and their perfect wickedness. There are condescending academics and NGOers who, without understanding a fraction of what Juan does, have built a career off pity, rendering gang members as perfect victims. The complexity of gangs—and the people who join them—is all too often cast aside. Much nonsense has been written on Mara Salvatrucha. It will keep being written, as long as pizzeria journalists lack the understanding or motivation to dig deeper.

Juan has a way with words. Don't take my word for it; you hold the proof in your hands. Juan's writing has appeared in leading publications and he has researched MS for decades. He continues doing so now. At present, he is working on a biography of an ex-member of MS, an ex-hitman for MS, a *traitor* to MS. He has worked on this story for two years, during which time he's traveled to the hideout of the man with a bounty on his head.

MS matters in Central America—no one argues otherwise—but it also matters in Mexico, and plays a huge role in the lives of many Latinx communities in the United States. MS is an international brand that even now is attempting to open branches in Spain. The emergence of MS is testimony to the failure of states to deal with aimless and disenfranchised young men. It is this failure which led to the emergence of a gang of killers. *See, Hear, and Shut Up* is an insider's view into MS. When you read this book, you will not be watching events unfold from the balcony; rather, you will be transported there, front and center, as scary as that may be. Still, that is not the strongest argument for reading it. The strongest argument is Juan's madness and tenacity. It is the tenacity of a man who mounts a motorcycle to a fearsome neighborhood time and time again, without being paid a cent, because he thinks what he is about to explain can change things. The strongest argument is that this madness—or this benevolence, whatever you may choose to call it—much like good books on MS, is rare in this world.

# Introduction

THE ACCOUNTS IN this book concern the last link of a chain of events and sociocultural processes that began long ago, and quite far from the marginal towns of El Salvador. To better understand this requires a dizzying trip through history and through the Americas. This book focuses on the life of members of an MS-13 clica in San Salvador, on the community they govern and their savage war on the young men of the Barrio 18 gang. However, a great deal had to take place before these young men would choose to mark their bodies with the two letters[1] and dedicate their lives to one of the largest gangs in the world. A great many contingencies and coincidences had to transpire, as did injustices and inequalities, for the two largest gangs in the Americas to become enmeshed in the most brutal gang conflict in recent history.

In 1938, the German writer Carl Stephenson published a short story, "Leiningens Kampf mit den Ameisen," that talks about the life of a millionaire who funds a cacao plantation in the Amazon rainforest. His dream is cut short by an invasion of millions of ants

---

1    In Spanish, "*las dos letras*"—slang for the initials MS.

that destroy everything and, ultimately, consume Leiningen himself. The story was wildly popular, and was translated into English as "Leiningen Versus the Ants." Some years later, the director Byron Haskin adapted the story for film. The tale was diluted, and reappeared in 1954 under the name *The Naked Jungle*, starring Charlton Heston. It was a box office hit. The film did not reach El Salvador until the 1960s, under the name *When the Army Roars (Cuando Ruge la Marabunta)*. In the movie, Heston fights to defend his estate from the millions of ants that seek to devour it.

The film's success in El Salvador was so great that it transformed the word from its title describing the plague of ants, *marabunta*, into a term used to refer to a group of friends, a crowd, or the masses. In this way, *marabunta* became simply, *mara*. The word *mara* quickly became a part of everyday slang, but it didn't yet have a negative connotation. *Mara* defined a group of friends just as easily as it did a rambunctious group of strangers.

The 1960s saw a great deal of changes across the country. It was then that insurgent groups began to take power. It was then that the idea of armed struggle against a military regime began to take root in the heads of intellectuals and workers. However, it wasn't until 1975 that the first groups capable of truly disrupting the state took form. Things quickly went downhill, culminating in a bloody civil war.[2] Counterinsurgent repression was increasingly cruel (and, with help from the US government, increasingly sophisticated as well). By 1979, the disappeared (*desaparecidos*) racked up in the hundreds. The conflict claimed the lives of youths, whether recruited by the army or pulled into guerillas to fight the *enemy*. It was in this context

---

2    Galeas Giovani, *Heroes Under Suspicion* (San Salvador: Athenas, 2013).

that countless Salvadorans fled—some under threat from paramilitary groups, others from sheer terror at the prospect of facing armed conflict. They sought refuge in countries like Sweden, Australia, Canada, and Costa Rica; but above all they went toward the United States, particularly Los Angeles, California, which by then was known as a mecca for gangs.

Salvadorans made up one of the youngest migrant groups in Los Angeles, decades after Mexicans who arrived as informal workers at the end of the nineteenth century and again through the *bracero* program in the 1940s. The Salvadorans who thought of California as the land of milk and honey did not take long to find that California waged a different sort of war. Hundreds of Chicano gangs[3] fought amongst themselves for control of territory, to secure status and run the streets. They, too, fought against gangs of other ethnicities—African Americans, Anglos, and Asians—who expressed through their conflicts the racial shocks and immense competition imposed upon migrants and other marginalized peoples.

The Salvadorans faced great challenges to adapting. Discrimination by the older, more established migrants was brutal, and like rocks that through sheer pressure become diamonds, the community found itself stronger and more cohesive throughout California's cities. Anthropologist Tom Ward traced the first predecessors to Mara Salvatrucha in the late 1970s,[4] groups of

---

3     Chicano culture exists as a hybrid. Neither Mexican nor Anglo, it is a culture that melds values, norms, and conceptions from both sides to create a set of values all its own.

4     Tom Ward, *Gangster Without Borders: An Ethnography of a Salvadoran Street Gang* (London: Oxford University Press, 2012).

young Salvadorans, first generation migrants who'd been raised in the Salvador of repression, who now took refuge with their families in California. They had long hair, wore black, and listened to black metal. They weren't a gang in the Angeleno sense of the word, though they had rivalries with groups like them including The Mob Crew, or TMC, and the Rebels or Crazy Riders, gangs who were also associated with a particular musical genre.

It was then, in this pressure cooker of marginalization, that the word *mara* came to be used to describe Salvadorans and became a symbol of their identity. A word that still resonated among those from its place of origin, that evoked El Salvador. This, according to anthropologist Abilio Vergara,[5] is one of the central aims of slang: to distinguish oneself from others, to create an intangible barrier placing some within and some without. In this way, these groups of Salvadoran youth became known as the Mara Salvatrucha Stoners. *Salvatrucha*, slang for Salvadoran identity, and *stoners* for their punk affinities. Between 1979 and 1983, disparate groups of Salvadoran stoners began to intermingle, to standardize initiation rituals and to clash—each time more fiercely—with other Hispanic gangs. The group lacked Chicanismo, and clashed with other gangs in terms of both aesthetics and lifestyle. The shaved heads and loose pants, which were the hallmarks of older gangs like White Fence 13, Hawaiian Gardens 13, Artesia 13, or Barrio 38 were a far cry from the long hair, skinny jeans, and black shirts favored by the Mara Salvatrucha Stoners.

---

5   Abilio Vergara, *Dentro de los túneles de sentido: Violencia, imaginarios, organización social, rituales y lenguaje en las pandillas juveniles de Ayacucho, Perú* (Mexico: ENAH, 2010).

These other gangs had been in the state for decades. Some were founded by migrant Mexicans in the 1920s and had weaved a complex system of alliances and social expectations with other Latino gangs.[6] This system, which still eluded the MSS (Mara Salvatrucha Stoners) in the early 1980s, originated in the mid-twentieth century when Chicano gang members in Southern California decided to create, from a variety of gangs, an exclusive prison gang. It was something akin to the national team picking standout players from a handful of soccer teams. After an explosive power grab within the California prison system, the group took the name The Mexican Mafia, or La Eme (M); they also identified with the number 13, as M is the thirteenth letter of the alphabet. It is for this reason that Chicano gangs in Southern California add a 13 to their names—as a sign of deference to the gang of gangs that rules the streets from inside prison.[7]

By the mid-'80s, a mass of members had landed in prison due to brawls with other gangs, armed theft, drug trafficking, and the like. Slowly they began to absorb the Chicano lifestyle. As their sentences drew to an end, this transformation began to take shape on the streets, such that by 1986 the gang was known as Mara Salvatrucha 13. Now a prominent figure in Southern California's gang landscape, they began to draw the attention of rival gangs.

They were playing a dangerous game, and it didn't take long to make enemies of nearly every gang in their path. They were

---

6   Marco Lara Klahr, *Hoy te toca la muerte: El imperio de las maras visto desde dentro* (Mexico: Planeta, 2006).

7   Chris Blatchford, *The Black Hand: The Story of Rene "Boxer" Enriquez and His Life in the Mexican Mafia* (New York: HarperCollins, 2008).

playing the game in earnest, whatever the cost. Several had been members of the armed forces or guerillas in El Salvador, and few had been untouched by violence back home. They had little to fear from their rivals: "They think they know about violence? We'll show those bitches what violence is!"[8] The gang had emerged, hungry and fearless.

Faced with war on many different fronts, a single gang helped to foster MS-13 in its growth within California's gang landscape. It was an old gang from the 1970s, once made up of Mexicans and Chicanos, but it had later grown lax in its ethnic prerequisites and let Filipinos, Caribbeans, and Central Americans join its ranks. The Eighteenth Street Gang, or Barrio 18, partnered with MS-13 for a time, like sister organizations. This allowed MS-13's clicas to grow and gain control of territories under the watchful eye of their mentors. New clicas began to emerge, like the Normandie Locos Salvatrucha, the Hollywood Locos Salvatrucha, the Leeward Locos Salvatrucha, and the Coronado Locos Salvatrucha, among many others. Their symbols marked the streets, and their names invoked fear and respect backed by machetes, bullets, and brutality.

The alliance with Barrio 18 was fractured at a party in 1988 near Martin Luther King Boulevard in South Los Angeles. It is not clear what happened, but some veterans say a spat between Popeye, from the western cell, with an 18er called Boxer, was to blame. Others say it was revenge for the beating of an 18er known as Pony, who was formerly in MS-13. There are others who say it was caused by payback for a cheating wife. Whatever it was, following the spat, members of Barrio 18 drove by and unloaded their bullets into Shaggy of

---

8    A quote from a veteran member of MS-13.

the Western Locos Salvatrucha clica. What *is* known is that Shaggy bled out that night, and since then, the war between the two has been unrestrainable.

Meanwhile in El Salvador, the civil war that had embroiled the country in the '80s came to an end on January 16, 1992. The country was in ruins, its infrastructure reduced to rubble, its social fabric irremediably torn. El Salvador was a country of orphans, of the unemployed, the crippled and maimed. And while the state tried to pick up the pieces, army combatants and guerillas alike found themselves out of work.

In this lawless terrain, bands of kidnappers and assassins were on fertile ground.[9] Neighborhood gangs proliferated. And, in a twist of irony, the US government then decided to deport hundreds of gang members from the state of California. They were mostly young men, members of Mara Salvatrucha 13 and Barrio 18. Many had migrated in their teenage years or younger, and returned to El Salvador as men. The only thing uniting them was their knowledge of California's gang ecosystem, and their time spent in prison. They descended like predators, like ants in a colony. They consumed everything in their path. Piecemeal neighborhood gangs saw no choice but to join one of the two for their own survival. The alternative was complete annihilation. MS-13 and Barrio 18 proliferated with such astounding force that before long not a single street corner went unclaimed. Homicide rates skyrocketed, and quickly became among the highest on the continent. Another war had begun, but this one would last far longer.

---

9    Hector Silva Ávalos, *Infiltrados: Cronica de la corrupción de la PNC (1992–2013)* (San Salvador: UCA Editores, 2014).

Members of MS-13 established the clicas they had belonged to up north, like Hollywood Locos Salvatrucha and Fulton Locos Salvatrucha. However, with the passage of time, newer, more localized clicas emerged. The two primary Salvadoran clicas of Mara Salvatrucha 13 formed—Sansivar Locos Salvatrucha and Harrison Locos Salvatrucha—quite likely the first outside the United States. Hundreds of groups followed.

In the suburbs of Mejicanos, one of the capital's most populous and dangerous barrios, Guanacos Criminales Salvatrucha was founded in 1999. Since then, they have run the place. Concurrently, MS-13 GCS took root along the hillsides, with Columbia Little Sycos del Barrio 18 dominating a strip along the outskirts of La Montreal, at the base of the hillside.[10] It was here, by the hill, that I first had the chance to live among members of MS-13 while conducting anthropological research on gang violence. From January to December 2010 I documented the war between these two groups and came to know the lives of the people caught in the crossfire. This book is a snapshot in time—a collection of field notes throughout the course of my research that served as the basis for my academic work. It must be said that this is not a strictly academic book. But it's also not a novella. All that has been written here is true, and it was subject to the strictest ethnographic standards. It approximates what the late anthropologist Oscar Lewis called *ethnographic realism.*

I leave it for you to judge these people in the last neighborhood on the hill.

---

10  A neighborhood in Mejicanos.

# Field Notes: The Last Neighborhood on the Hill

THIS PROBABLY ISN'T the best day to start my research. It's the eighteenth. A bad omen for MS-13. On this day, Barrio 18 tends to avenge its dead—those killed by MS just five days before, on the thirteenth.

As we approach the last neighborhood on the hill, our escort watches us like a hawk. He leaves us in the care of another pair of eyes that repeat the process.

"A little faster if you can, brother."

It is Marcos, riding in tow on the cheap Chinese motorcycle that serves as our transportation. I push the motor until it is spewing exhaust, groaning with each pothole. And Marcos repeats, trying to hide his nerves:

"Maybe a little faster, still. Once we're a little higher up we can slow down."

Our surroundings have a rural air. Bucolic, really. Dirt roads, and brick houses with fiber cement for roofing. You can still see hints of the cardboard shacks they once were. If not for the graffiti, it would look like an average neighborhood on the fringe of some city.

The rainy season has yet to arrive, but every so often we come across pools of stagnant water. Pools that in winter become a rushing river, threatening to sweep up any living thing in the area.

"This isn't even the worst of it. Around there is where they'd toss the bodies," reports Marcos, livening our ascent up the hill. He is a young man, some nineteen years old. He has lived here all his life. His brother was a member of Mara Salvatrucha and he knows these roads like the back of his hand. He guides me through this hell like Dante's Virgil, and I, clumsy and scared, follow his instructions to a T. If he tells me not to look in some direction, I don't; if he tells me to speed up, I do so without asking questions.

"Slow down now, we're in the Salvatrucha zone," he says, and by his tone I gather that this is supposed to be reassuring.

Block by block, the walls start to show MS-13 graffiti painted in black or blue. As we draw closer, the signs, walls, and sidewalks announce to us that the brothers of MS-13 live here.

We reach our destination, the last neighborhood on the hill. We are greeted by a large gang mural, guarded by a handful of young men who, upon seeing us, stand defiantly. Marcos greets them. They look us over and return to their posts without greeting us back. Like old hens, they watch over their roost.

I am here to do field work for an anthropological thesis on violence in El Salvador, specifically that which results from a war between the two biggest gangs in America: Mara Salvatrucha and Barrio 18. Their conflict has endured for decades, and traversed continents. The whys of this war between babes is what brings me here.

Two months ago I started knocking on doors of NGOs that work with gang members, looking for an in. One by one, I was turned down and told that the situation was too complicated.

Finally, after a long search, I found a priest who was willing to help me. The institution he heads has operated in the area for years and has contacts with the gang on the hill. They run a youth center at the top of the hill, and this is precisely where Marcos guides me now.

The house is large, and it is near the outskirts of the community, just toward the end of the only road that leads there. At the entrance, we find Gustavo painting colored letters on the wall. He is in charge of the center. He's young, somewhere between twenty-five and thirty. He walks and talks as if he were on a beach somewhere. It seems as if nothing and no one can get under his skin.

With that same serene affect, he tells me the priest had spoken about me and asks what I hope to learn. I babble on about my theoretical lens, my methodological schema and hypothesis.

Nothing. Just silence.

He crosses his arms and asks, "So you want to, like, meet the gang members? There's a bunch here, but they're easygoing."

"Yes . . . Something like that," I answer.

He tells me if I would like to remain alive throughout the course of my study, there are several things I should know and several rules I should follow:

The first is strict: *I am to never, under any circumstances, mention the number 18, or wear shirts that bear those digits.*

In a place like this, it seems, that number draws death like a moth to a flame.

*I shouldn't walk alone.* They don't know me, and they might confuse me for an enemy.

Marcos agrees with a nervous nod of the head. They tell me that the last novitiate who neglected the rule was intercepted by a gang in transit and was forced to strip for a tattoo search.

Gustavo scans me from head to toe, and disapproves.

"No, you can't be coming like this, it's dangerous."

He means my earring and haircut. He says I should look more formal, more serious.

Gustavo and I reach a deal. He'll let me visit the youth center and conduct my research here if I collaborate with him on his projects. Before leaving, Gustavo and Marcos whisper among themselves and then make me an offer I can't turn down.

"Listen, would you want to meet the guys who run this place now?"

I say yes, and they tell me to follow a protocol, as if they were taking a dangerous beast from its cage. They instruct me to avoid staring at their tattoos or asking them anything, just to introduce myself and leave.

Marcos walks to the backyard and returns a few minutes later accompanied by two men. They are both somewhere around thirty. One is tan, with a shaved head and a sparse mustache buttressed by tattoos. The other sports a light complexion and blond hair, and a gigantic MS tattooed on his forehead. He looks me up and down and extends his hand with a barely-hidden glare. They ask my name, tell me theirs and depart unhurriedly.

Tomorrow, Gustavo will be waiting for me at the bottom of the hill to make the ascent again at 7 a.m. As we depart, in front of the youth center I see an enormous mural with the initials GCS— Guanacos Criminales Salvatrucha—the clica that runs the highland.

Marcos and I mount the bike and take off. Bit by bit, we leave behind the dirt roads and graffiti, and again, my Virgil begs:

"Just a little bit faster, brother."

# The Broom of Truth (Which Sweeps Away the Lies)

IT IS 10 A.M. In the youth center's backyard, four gang members surround a girl of fifteen or so. She is seated in a plastic chair, and one of them looms before her with half a broomstick in his hands.

"No, no, noooo! I don't even know them. I don't even talk to them!" wails the girl. Her cry is immediately followed by a dry thud.

"Nooo! I don't even know them, I barely talk to them."

The pattern repeats. A grunt, a blow, then more of the same:

"Noooo! I didn't tell them anything, I didn't say anything, I don't even know them!"

A teenager wields the stick. He is tan, with a large gold earring in each ear and a beard dripping with beads of sweat. He takes off his shirt and ambles before the girl, still wielding the stick. When he spots me, he cocks his head and scowls, like a dog baring his teeth. He doesn't say anything, but his look says it all. The other three surround the girl and ask questions. They beat her without waiting for answers. Gustavo comes out from his office and approaches to watch the girl's trial. He pretends to grab something and signals with his eyes that I should follow him to his office. Once there, he tells me to be more careful: seeing too much can be dangerous. He says the center's previous employee had to leave due to gang threats. Apparently he didn't understand the region's guiding law: *See, Hear, and Shut Up.*

Today we ascended the hill early. Gustavo picked me up in a car from the center. The journey is far more peaceful than last time. At this time of day, we see no gang members, and gone are the wary stares. The youth center is a large building with three rooms, a gigantic kitchen space, and a back patio. It is not the most welcoming place, despite Gustavo's efforts. Colorful posters adorn the walls, but even so, the menace is palpable. It seems that every youth who has passed through here has left a mark: the floor is covered in grime; the walls are marked with shoe prints, hearts bearing initials, and MS graffiti.

On the patio, the blond gangster is tidying up. He left prison a few months ago and, when he's not crashing with other gang members, he sleeps in the youth center. I take a broom and help him. His hearing is bad, and I nearly have to shout to get him to understand me. He seems laid back. Every so often he takes a break and scans the mountaintops. We talk about anything. He tells me about his pet, a fighting dog, how cold it is in these hills at night, how annoying it is to sneak around during National Civil Police (PNC) patrols. He sprinkles his phrases with *thank you, please,* and *god willing,* like he's making an effort to show manners. He finishes cleaning up and sits in a plastic chair, then begins sketching a tattoo. He goes by Destino,[11] and I am told he's one of the founders of this clica, and its current leader.

---

11  In English, Destiny.

As the day goes on, a procession of gang members arrives at the youth center. They greet us brusquely and head to the patio where Destino awaits, seated on the plastic chair. They approach him, whisper in his ear, and depart in a rush.

Piece by piece, the patio becomes something of an office. Destino's two cell phones don't give him a moment of peace. He sits there on his throne of plastic, spending his day like Al Pacino in *The Godfather*. He gets up only to make space for the four gang members and the frightened girl they drag in their wake.

It is lunchtime, and as we eat some instant soup with Destino, one of the young men who tormented the girl approaches us. Like everyone, he approaches my host with respect, and a certain submission. In what I think is an attempt at ingratiating himself, he slides me a dollar on the chair.

"Here, so you can get yourself a soda."

I obey. Not five minutes later, I am pouring glasses of foamy Salva Cola. This gangster is short and dark, with lively eyes. He wears a tight-fitting black jersey and black Nike sneakers. He is jittery, and scans in every direction like a human motion sensor. I later find out he's a hitman for the Guanacos Criminales Salvatrucha *clica*, and that a few days prior he shot two young men to death in the foothills of the mountain. The girl he tormented is one of his girlfriends. Other gangsters arrive at the patio and speak in slang I can scarcely make out. Some watch me with mistrust, others couldn't care less, but either way I decide it's best to draw back and let them talk. I go out to buy cigarettes.

The main street, the only one that goes here, is quiet at this hour. From here you can see it wind up and down the mountain. People move slowly. Some women balance pitchers and baskets on their heads. A real feat on this incline.

Soon I encounter a gang member. He sports a green jersey down to his wrists, from which you can see a mass of black tattoos poking out. As he spots me, he slows his pace and stares. I have never seen him but he seems to know me. I ask if he has a cigarette, or knows where I can find a store.

"Oh, you want cigs. Sure. I don't smoke, but gimme a sec, I'll have some *bolo*[12] run out."

He scans his surroundings, and addresses a man. He is old and tattered, and clearly pushing his lungs to make the incline.

"Hey! You, bolo. Go get this man some cigs."

The man looks back at the hill he has just conquered, and with resignation in his voice, asks:

"Menthol or no?"

---

12  Slang for drunkard in El Salvador.

# Destino's Rent[13]

THE AIR IS TENSE in the last neighborhood on the hill. Last night, the police captured several members of Destino's clica on a raid. Members of Guanacos Criminales Salvatrucha come and go at the youth center without acknowledging me or Gustavo, who is wholly immersed in a giant jigsaw puzzle, pausing only occasionally to check that no piece has made its way to the floor.

Amidst the chaos enters Hugo. He is a kid, twelve years old, with big eyes that scrunch when he laughs. He orbits the gangsters like a satellite; he's one of Destino's protégés.

Hugo makes a joke and Destino bursts into laughter. Seconds later, the gangsters join in. The only one who is not laughing is Little Down. He's in his chair, with a face like stone. He runs his fingers along his chains then gets up and sits next to me. Little Down and I talk for a bit, and after exchanging a few anecdotes and our phone numbers, he leaves. Just like yesterday, he's dressed in black, and when he walks down the main street people avert their eyes and

---

13  This term refers to extortion in the form of the weekly payments small businesses pay to gangs. This occurs throughout the country.

speed up their pace. Little Down walks nervously, and his clutch of amulets announce his presence with a clinking.

Meanwhile, at the youth center, two women lean against the door. They ask me to call Destino, and he grudgingly gets up from his throne. They talk for a bit, like they are haggling almost. One is young and thin, with two girls furled up in her skirt. A third child walks with zombie-like conviction toward Gustavo's jigsaw puzzle. Gustavo refuses to share his treasure, giving her a forbidding glare. The other woman is fat and several years older than the first. After a bit, the monarch grabs a handful of bills and gives them to her. Gustavo glances at me, then explains to me that their boyfriends/husbands are gangsters who are now locked up; they come to Destino every few months asking for money. The women don't leave, they keep haggling and soon enough they receive another handful of bills. They both hug him, kiss him on the cheeks, and leave content with their spoils. Gustavo has finished his puzzle. He shows it to me proudly, then rushes off to hide it in the office. On his face, the unmistakable grin of a job well done.

Destino remains by the doorway. He sees the two women saunter off with their money. He puts a hand in his pocket, stares intently at the coins he has left, and grumbles:

"And they say gangsters don't get extorted."

# Karla's Crime

IT IS 2 P.M. and the heat has imposed a curfew. The neighborhood is still. My little bike's wheels struggle not to get caught in the loose dirt, which in turn uses my back as its own canvas. Everything in the neighborhood is covered with dust, from the leaves on the trees to the people. Suddenly, a soldier appears, like a mirage. He walks alone, with a military march and his hand on the trigger of an M16. He looks in each direction and discretely signals with his rifle to each person he sees. He must be trailing behind from the convoys that ascend the hill daily. He is headed in the opposite direction and as our paths cross I can see a panicked look on his face. We pass and he's lost in the dust.

The last neighborhood on the hill is the same as ever; everyone sleeps and the silence is heavy and contagious. The sun is merciless against the tin roofs, and makes puddles of stagnant water smell so pungent you can almost taste them. Inside the youth center I find Gustavo. He is speaking with two novitiates who have been sent to work here by their congregation.

In the backyard—Destino's office—there's a meeting. Two visitors have arrived to discuss something with the oldest members of the clica. At the meeting, besides Destino, is Dark, the gangster I met the first day; Little Down, the hitman; and El Maniaco,[14] who hit the girl with the broomstick some days ago. The two men have something to sell and they haggle with Guanacos Criminales Salvatrucha. They are both in their thirties. One is fat, with a cowboy mustache, and he tortures his belly with a football jersey that's stretched to its limit. He looks like a human meatball. The other is well dressed, sporting a button-down shirt to his wrists and charro boots. Suddenly, two kids appear with plates of food. They have bought them at the cafeteria in the foothills, right on the boundary of Mara Salvatrucha's territory. Each plate runs $3.50, a real luxury in these parts. The two men grab their plates and devour them before the greedy faces of the others. Every so often, El Maniaco moves his mouth like a fish, as if it were he who was eating. The visitors finish their lunch, dispose of their trash, and ask for cigarettes. The Guanacos zealously accommodate their every request. Only Little Down stays put. He's spread out in a plastic chair and looks at them defiantly, stroking his amulets.

In the streets, the sun at last takes mercy on us. People begin to leave their homes, children resume making a racket, and even the dogs, who just a few hours ago were like rugs in the street, come back to life. Hugo, Destino's protégé, sits by my side and breaks the silence every five minutes to ask me things.

"Is this motorcycle yours?"

"How do you drive it?"

"Can I touch it?"

He tells me his mother's name is Jazmín, and that she sells fruit juices in front of the communal home.

---

14  In English, The Maniac.

His sister is Karla, the girl the gang members tormented the other day with a broomstick. The crime that nearly cost Karla her life was bringing a friend over to her home. That, and nothing more. The problem is that her friend lives on the outskirts, in Barrio 18 territory. Karla's life was spared after her interrogation. However, the clica decided that she should no longer study. The school she attended also resides in enemy territory.

On the corner, a woman hawks bread, and people make their pilgrimage. As the evening sets in, you can hear the church hymns. There are several churches, and they fight amongst themselves to see who can most loudly proclaim their praise for God. It is a battle of decibels. Gustavo closes the youth center and Guanacos Criminales Salvatrucha exit alongside their two visitors. Surely they have made good deals. The strange men hop in a car and speed down the hill. Night has fallen, and Destino and his gangsters sit out on a street corner to smoke weed and flirt with the handful of admirers surrounding them.

At the end of the street, the Catholic community prepares to face the sonic assault of the evangelicals. They are a troop of old women who pray the rosary and sing psalms. But try as they may, they can't compete with the howls of pastors who with every shout seem to confront all the devils of hell and Lucifer himself.

It is late, and it's time for me to go.

On the way down, near the bottom of the hill, a police patrol has stopped a caravan. They illuminate the faces of the riders from the bed of the pickup, and one of them yells something at the conductor. Inside, people look calm, they look at the scene with resignation.

# Omens of War

IT IS NOON and the aura of lunch trails through the neighborhood. The scent is a mix of instant soup, eggs, beans, and tortillas, many tortillas, freshly made. At this hour, the community is staunchly divided between the haves and have-nots. What determines who resides in which group is ultimately arbitrary. If you earned something that morning you eat lunch. If not, better wait for dinner— that is, if the afternoon is more productive. If by nightfall there's still nothing to add to the pot of boiling water, well, maybe tomorrow will be a better day.

The first group, the haves, takes refuge in their homes to cook what they have procured, supplementing with water if it's not enough. The second group, the have-nots, is comprised of the drunks and the vagrants, some kids who sniff around from their windows, and those whose morning has left them with nothing but hopes for a better afternoon. On the patio of the youth center, Destino has left his plate half-eaten and speaks with the two mysterious men who were here yesterday. It seems they have come to hand over what Destino haggled for so insistently. The one who looks like a Mexican cowboy is nervous, he stomps his boots and wiggles his cigarette between his fingers.

"Destino, they should post up. Have the dawgs posted up, yeah?" he says, signaling toward the mountaintop and toward the street leading down the hill.

"Of course!" answers Destino, as if offended by the remark.

At present, Guanacos Criminales Salvatrucha are spread thin. They have been patrolling the community and the hills that surround it since morning. They go in groups. At a distance, I can make out El Maniaco. He is posted at the entrance to the community with a hand tucked underneath his shirt. At his side is Bernardo, an aspiring gangster. He has tried to join the clica for a few months, but up until now he's only managed to get insignificant jobs. He is tall and thin, must be fifteen or so, and with a face covered in acne he's the spitting image of adolescence.

El Noche,[15] the gangster who sent a drunkard down the hill to get me cigarettes, walks along a small patrol of young men. He sports a polo down to his elbows, leaving his tattoo-covered forearms in full view. He walks by me and flashes the Salvatrucha claw[16] in greeting. The last in his squad is Moxy, another wannabe gangster. He splits off from the group to touch my motorcycle.

"Damn! This bike is crazy. Man, I can drive these and even bigger ones. Just ask Little Down, I've taken him way out."

El Noche shoots him a stony look and Moxy resumes his place in the troop that's soon out of sight.

---

15  In English, The Night.

16  The gang's token hand symbol is a claw.

Little Down doesn't patrol. He assists Destino in his bargaining with the cowboy. Soon enough, the two men take a black bag from a trunk and pass it along. Inside is something round and heavy, like a mango. When it's Little Down's turn to scope out the purchase, he grins. He looks like a kid with a new toy.

"Hey dawgs, come take the goods!" yells Destino, and a pack of gangsters grab the bag before disappearing into the streets.

It is almost 3 p.m., and the neighborhood slowly comes to life. The sun gleams off the tin roofs and distorts the shadows. The sound of reggaeton rebounds through the streets and mingles with a chorus of shouts from the old man on the corner, who, they say, was driven mad by a witch.

At the youth center, Destino, the visitors, and some gangsters are seated on the steps and amusedly watch a small spectacle. Hugo, who's been gone all afternoon, is badgering Moxy with jocular punches. He is intent on keeping the spotlight, and each time Destino explodes into laughter. Moxy smiles nervously but grimaces when the child delivers a new blow to his ribs. He looks at the rest as if to say, "Okay, that's enough." But the Guanacos Criminales Salvatrucha crew are entertained, and Hugo shows no signs of stopping.

Destino's clica is getting ready for something. New members are being admitted, and they are getting the necessary supplies to begin their adventure. A few days ago, in downtown San Salvador, an M67 industrial grenade blew four members of Barrio 18 to pieces, and others still have detonated throughout the country. The residents on the mountain know how to read these signs, and get ready for war. Shops close early, people walk more hurriedly, avoiding eye contact, and homes shut down like small bunkers at night. There is an air of death throughout the hillside.

# The Mara's Clowns

"EY, YOU EAT yet, dawg?"

This is Destino's greeting to each gangster after flashing the Salvatrucha claw.

At my right, seated, is El Noche, who shows off his new cell phone and heckles Tombo,[17] a gangster from another clica who has come to bolster Guanacos Criminales Salvatrucha. At my left are Hugo and Moxy, the latter still sore from the former's playful—but prolonged—beating. Behind us, Little Down scolds someone over the phone. Before us, Destino unpacks bags of food, and all of us, tortillas in hand, descend upon the plates. More than eat, we *defile* the chorizo, rice, and chicken, which are soon reduced to scraps. Little Down, despite our insistence, refuses to eat. He watches us with a paternal air, with a certain contempt. Suddenly he gets up and tosses a liter of Salva Cola at us, and human piranhas that we are, we glug it down fervently. It is the first meal of the day.

---

17  Slang for police officer.

The routine is straightforward, gangsters toss in bills and coins in a pile, then send novices to get food from the outskirts of town. It is a risky job. Down at the base of the hill lives Barrio 18, and one has to cross directly in front of the police station. Soldiers, too, patrol the area. It's a dangerous business, getting lunch. Most of all because those who get sent are the novices. However, since they are novices, they're not recognized, they don't have much *bray*.[18] Neither the cops nor Barrio 18 associate them with MS. When the food arrives, it's a party, everyone grabs a tortilla and eats what they can. It doesn't matter how much or how many gangsters are around, everyone gets at least a bite.

Hugo looks at me with his mouth full and smiles. The plates start to empty, and the Salva Cola is replaced by loud belches. Cigarettes for the last course.

"Look, man, fuck! So a while back I dressed up as a clown, man, for a nephew's birthday party," says Moxy to El Noche, and begins his anecdote.

His story is good, though a little exaggerated, and he steals a chuckle from the group. But Little Down has a better story to tell.

"I dressed up like a clown once too, man. Ha! Bro, but just to kill some dumbshit. Fuckin' face paint and all, I went, and the dude's like, 'Hey, look, a clown!' Then he hesitates a sec, and looks at me, and I just tell him, 'Later, bro,' and BAM! BAM! BAM! He took like ten gunshots to the face. I left that dumbass in the street."

This is how clown stories end in Mara Salvatrucha.

---

18  A word used by gangsters to refer to those who are wanted. Also used to refer to those on the radar of police.

# We're Bad[19]

IT'S EARLY, AND the day is warm and muggy. The sun hasn't risen quite yet. Drops of dew tremble on leaves, and the people who live in the last neighborhood on the hill begin their pilgrimage to the streets, to scrape something together for mealtime.

Fifty feet from the youth center, a man lays on the sidewalk with his head burst open, a panicked expression still visible on his face despite the four gunshots he took. They killed him a while ago and his body still bleeds.

I'm standing in front of the body alongside another curious few, mostly women and children. They just stand there, with no mention of the killing. Some gossip, others talk about their sales the day before, kids run and play near their mothers.

---

19  In reference to "Semos Malos," a short story by Salvadoran author Salvador Salazar Arrué (1899–1975), known as Salarrué. It tells the tale of a father and son, two rural peasants in search of a better life. They attempt to sell a phonograph, but on their way are intercepted and killed by a group of bandits. The bandits play music on the phonograph and are moved to tears, closing with the phrase: "We're bad."

People gather like it's the entrance to a circus. Among the women is Jazmín, Hugo's mother, who places a large crate on the ground and strokes a baby carried by a young woman.

The police arrive, unhurriedly. Four fat men who walk lethargically toward the corpse, stopping to stretch or yawn once in a while. They fill out a form, put up yellow tape, and call for a patrol.

The cops are waiting on the forensics team and the detectives. Both take a while to show up. When they greet each other they exchange jokes, and it seems they go way back. Suddenly, a news truck appears. Now that everyone has arrived they begin the gruesome display.

"Let's start, then," says one of the investigators, and the corpse is photographed by the cops and detectives. They move him from side to side looking for shell casings, search his pockets.

"Check him for drugs," says one, filling out paperwork.

Nothing in his pockets, just a few coins, barely enough for bus fare.

"Tattoos!" he cries.

Two men lift his shirt, drop his pants, check his hands and neck, but still, nothing. People watch the scene in silence. With each thrust, more blood spills, prompting murmurs from nearby children.

Beside the corpse, a bag drips with blood.

"Ey! Check the bag. Make sure there's no weapons in there," says the cop, and the clang of metal rings out as it is opened. One by one, his weapons are displayed victoriously: a hammer, a handsaw, a screwdriver, a handful of nails . . .

The man was the neighborhood carpenter. He was waiting for the bus when one of the Guanacos Criminales Salvatrucha gave him four blasts to the face. No one knows quite who it was or why. No one wants to know, it seems, including the police.

People begin to disperse, and the cops search the body like they are rifling through trash. The journalists struggle to park in a tiny space. A man wielding a camera approaches. With every step, a gush of sweat and a chorus of curses. Behind him steps a young lady with a microphone. She is well dressed, and stamps the dirt with her heels. She stands out like a penguin in the desert.

"Do you know the motive for the crime? Do you know the deceased?" she asks the crowd.

Nothing, silence.

Suddenly: "No, we don't know anything. I was inside when it happened."

That's the most she'll get.

The woman drops the microphone, disappointed, while the man points the camera toward the corpse. He holds it there for a while, like he's expecting it to do something.

The war has begun. The Guanacos Criminales Salvatrucha have retreated to the youth center. They are nervous, and their phones won't stop ringing. This place is becoming a barracks. The youngest of the bunch are quiet, and you can see the fear in their eyes. Others, now accustomed to war, joke around and speak animatedly. Destino and Little Down confer in the kitchen. As I walk in, Destino runs to greet me and hands me a chair with exaggerated politeness. I look at the young men surrounding me and think that any one of them could have killed that carpenter a few hours ago. I search their faces, and I don't spot a trace of culpability or remorse. They are used to this. It's not their first rodeo. Less than a month ago, a car made its way up the hill and peppered two young men with bullets. They both survived, one with deep cuts up his abdomen, the other left castrated by bullets. It's said it was Barrio 18, who, like Guanacos, have taken over territory in the area. Their kingdom is made up of Polanco, Jardín, and El Hoyo. Just a few blocks from Buenos Aires. The clica in question dons the pompous name Columbia Little Sycos-Tiny Locos. This is in stark contrast to their members, who, like Guanacos, they are mostly young men under twenty years of age.

It is said, too, that the Guanacos are preparing for vengeance. It's early evening, and the crime scene is now abandoned. A woman scrubs blood off the pavement and a few feet away, Jazmín has set up her juice stand. The community returns to its routine state of anxiety. One woman cries alone, withered and old, on the pavement. Her cries are bitter, and she gasps for breath between wails. She covers her face with her hands, which drip wet with tears. At her side, a younger woman consoles her and strokes her hair.

"It's okay, he's with God now, he's resting now," she says, as the carpenter makes his way downhill in a body bag.

# The Legend

DESTINO SITS IN his plastic chair and eyes the group. They are all teenagers. Some have already been initiated, others are hopeful recruits. Among them are Bernardo, El Chele, and Hugo, the youngest hopeful. This isn't a formal meeting, just Destino regaling the rookies with MS lore.

"Back in my old clica there was this homeboy by the name of El Demonio. That dude was crazy, had a pact with the devil," says Destino, spitting at the ground. He takes his shirt off to display his tattoos. The young men's eyes light up like full moons, and silence reigns.

"That vato, when we'd meet, he'd say, 'Is everyone here yet?' And we'd say yeah, then he'd move his arms and all the branches on the trees would move. It scared the shit out of us. When the cops would show, we'd all take off running, but him, man, just nothing. 'Ey, why you guys hiding?' he'd ask us, and walk by with two guns, one in each hand. 'Ey, wassup, are you guys looking for me?' he'd ask the cops. 'No, no, Demonio, just a routine check.' they'd answer. And they'd leave with their tails between their legs, fuckers.

"In prison, homeboy turned Christian, and the demons would torture him at night, for real. Other homeboys didn't believe it. But me, I knew how he was. He said they wouldn't let him rest, that they'd show up at night and jump on the beds. One time I was there and I heard them, they were jumping. No shit, they were jumping. Sometimes, in his cell, the devil would come and try to reclaim homeboy's soul. They say you could just see these footprints, like a bear's, and it smelled like shit. For real, it was the devil who wanted that vato's soul."

The young men are amazed, and Destino sits back in his chair with a look of satisfaction on his face.

In the war between gangs there is not only death and destruction, there are also small periods of calm. Today, for example, has been quiet, and the neighborhood seems at peace. The gangsters are holed up in the youth center, and they don't seem to be planning anything. I just stick around and listen. Some ask me things, nothing too deep; they want to know if the women in the University of El Salvador are attractive, if I don't get sick of studying, they want to know where I live and if the women there are attractive as well.

"Look Juan, in the Mara you can die for one of three reasons. For killing another homeboy, even if it's an accident, doesn't matter, whoever spills a homeboy's blood ain't worth shit. Those guys are fucked because MS wants them, the little bitches[20] want them, and the cops too. They're shit out of luck.

"You can die for being a snitch, for giving out information on what the gang's doing.

"And, you can die for being a faggot!"

---

20  MS tends to use this derogatory phrase to refer to its enemies in Barrio 18.

The hopefuls erupt into a chorus of laughter.

"Yeah, a faggot! If you're fucking a dude, you lower your prestige, and the gang's too. Damn, people will say, he couldn't even get a fat bitch, or an old-ass lady."

The speech is over and Destino puts his shirt back on, as if to indicate that the session is over.

Gustavo sits in the office. Though his role sounds prestigious—head of the youth center—his contribution up until now has been limited to opening up in the morning and locking up at night. A few days ago, Gustavo called out a gangster for coming in armed and smoking weed. The young man got heated, and only because Destino stepped in was a tragedy averted. Since then, Gustavo has kept to his office, sitting before an old computer with headphones on.

"Ey! Juan, I wanted to talk to you," he says as I pass by.

He explains that they have started a tutoring program for kids in the community, that he's been asked to make it happen. More concretely, he asks me to teach the kids in the afternoons. The tutoring will be held in a communal house, a big gloomy building. Right now, two novice teachers sent by the congregation teach there. But they just can't keep up. I agree to take on the job. I think it will give me the chance to study the upcoming war from a different angle.

"If you want, go scope it out, they're there now," he says, then plugs his headphones back in.

At the communal house, the two young teachers struggle with a herd of kids. Their inexperience shows. This is going to be a tough gig.

It's afternoon, and the sun bakes the mountaintop. A rush of wind drives away the heat for a few moments, at least. Those who headed out this morning make their way back, slowly scaling the hill. Those who have been lucky return with empty baskets. Others return carrying the merchandise they weren't able to sell. For the latter, dinner, if there is any, will be meager.

The Guanacos Criminales Salvatrucha gang has left the youth center and posted up on a corner to listen to music off Little Down's cell phone. The fun doesn't last long. From afar you can see a police patrol making its way up the hill. The gangsters return to their hideout.

Inside, El Noche gulps down a mango and Destino writes something in a notebook. Hugo has found a ball and practices his aim on the other gangsters, who accept his blows with resignation. Little Down is angry. He doesn't like having to hide from the cops. He tells me he'd rather face them up front, but now is not the time to make more enemies. He shoots Hugo a scathing look. Hugo sets aside the ball and takes refuge in view of Destino.

Night falls, and the aura of war is felt in the last neighborhood on the hill. Homes start to lock up, and those still in the streets speed up their pace. As I descend, I come across several patrols making their way up the hill. Once I reach ground level, down in Columbia Little Sycos territory, I'm followed by a fusillade of eyes, watching me like an enemy.

# The Game

TODAY IS MY first day as a tutor. To break the ice with the kids, I set up a game. Cops and robbers. As we split up into groups, they all ask to be robbers.

# No Men in the Garden

Today the calendar once again marks 18, and we in the last neighborhood on the hill are fearful. It's a heavy day. Even for those with no ties to Guanacos Criminales Salvatrucha, the enemy is one and the same: the Columbia Little Sycos from Barrio 18. The converse is true as well; people from here face suspicion downtown in Barrio 18 territory. This war divides all.

I am at the entrance to the communal home waiting for my students. One by one they arrive and get settled. I take a second to chat with Hugo and Karla's mother, Jazmín. She has spent several years selling drinks in these parts, and this war is nothing new to her.

"My husband, my kids' dad, got killed in 2006. I always think, if he were alive my kids wouldn't be how they are now. When he was around they still behaved. God, right now who knows where Karla is, I don't know if she's with that man or where the hell she went."

"What man?" I ask.

"That one, sir, Little Down. She's gone with him before. She was living in his house for a while, but look, she's a girl, she doesn't know how to wash men's clothes, or cook. At home, I do the cleaning, and I don't have her cook because she'll burn it. When I found out he beat her for not knowing that stuff, it made me furious. I went to talk to him. I didn't give a damn! 'Look,' I said. 'I don't give a damn who you are. If anything happens to her again, I won't let you get away with it.' I don't give a damn if I have to go into hiding! They're saying now it's him who's gonna run things around here, not Destino, I don't know. I don't give a damn, I'll do anything for my kids. 'Look,' I told Little Down. 'If their dad was here, you wouldn't be around anymore, just ask around what he was like. Ask.' I told him. Because look, Juan, their dad didn't fuck around."

"Why was he killed?" I ask.

"June fifth, they killed him. He had joined a crew. Not gang stuff, just a crew. Like, maybe he was short on cash. Like, you know, men with more than one girl don't have enough money, well, he had another wife and kids."

The kids have arrived and it's time for class to start. I leave Jazmín midway through our conversation.

Inside, the two seminarians are desperately trying to impose order. The ensemble of voices is unintelligible, like a horde of furious bees. In one corner, Kevin, a twelve-year-old, has one of the seminarians in a chokehold. He laughs, and calls the rest to show off his accomplishment. Seated at a table, a boy carves his initials on it with a three-inch pocketknife while the other kids run circles around the other seminarian, who pleads, like a broken record:

"Children, behave. Do your work."

I rush to free the first from Kevin's clutches, and he immediately replicates the chokehold on a classmate. I try to level with the kids who are running, but it's impossible. If I get Karen to sit, Melvin gets up and throws a notebook at Brian. If I, after much begging and pleading, get Cindy to do her work, Pamela tugs at my shirt crying because Alejandro has taken her things. And so on, and so on.

In a corner, a girl with big eyes and long, long black hair looks on at the rest with tears in her eyes.

"Nah, she's always like this. She's a weird one," says one of the seminarians when I ask about her.

I approach her slowly, sit by her side without saying a word, and she looks at me with terror in her face, braces herself, and lowers her eyes as if she were in the presence of a monster. She's not yet ten, her lips are painted bright red and she sports a miniskirt far too short for a girl.

"What's wrong, sweetie?" I ask gently.

The girl responds by pulling her skirt down, like she is hiding a treasure. She is consumed by anxiety. I ask if she wants to draw with me, and hand her a sheet of paper and some crayons. She doesn't answer, but she takes the crayons. She moves slowly, like she's afraid. Slowly, she starts to draw. I spend the afternoon by her side and manage to get a laugh out of her with my terrible drawings. A garden begins to emerge on her page. It is colorful, like a park. It is illuminated by a smiling sun, filled with swings and seesaws, with little girls running around throughout. In her drawing, all of the little girls are smiling. There are no men in her garden.

The session is over, and the bees swarm elsewhere. The girl stays behind, walking slowly with her drawing in her arms.

I stand in the doorway with a knot in my throat that won't let me breathe.

"Ey! Juan, are we playing or what?" yells one of the Guanacos Criminales Salvatrucha, bouncing a soccer ball on the dirt. I have forgotten completely. A few days ago I said I would play on the neighborhood field.

It is El Guapo[21] who beckons me, a gangster of some twenty years who stammers with every sentence. His description matches that of a suspect currently being blared on the news: black hair, dark eyes, five foot two, thin, tan, no tattoos.

I am scared, but I say yes. He says we'll hit the field that's lower down on the hill, and tells me not to worry, that it's not a serious game, just men in the neighborhood looking to kill time.

As we walk down the slope, a million news articles race through my head culminating in the same result: a group of young men murdered in a field on gang terrain. I am reminded, again and again, of today's date: February 18. The eighteenth of February. The eighteenth.

The gangster says we should cut through an alley down a slope filled with rocks and old tires. At the end of the slope lies a barren and dusty field. At the flanks, the men have improvised some bleachers with tires filled with cement and dirt. Dozens of MS and GCS clica murals envelop the area.

Several young men await the ball El Guapo holds in his hands. In a corner, on the grass, our team is waiting. Some stare at me with mistrust, others immediately launch into making jokes. Some tattoos peek through their clothing. I can't tell the gangsters and civilians apart. We form various teams of seven players. The team that gets scored on is replaced by another, tournament-style. And without further ado, we play.

In a lightning play, El Guapo sends the ball up the pitch and lands a corner kick. A tall, thin man goes for it, but misses. The

---

21  In English, The Handsome.

goalkeeper grabs the ball and sends it downfield. The others then run toward our goal, guarded only by this terrified anthropologist and a forty-something they call El Negro. He's our goalie. The opposing players advance ever closer, and my teammates call out:

"Let's go, man! Do it, fuck shit up!"

I face off against the forward who is a few feet in front of me, and launch myself toward the ball, eyes closed and bracing for impact. I hear a swoosh—the forward has taken a shot. I see nothing but a cloud of dust. I fear the worst. I get up and look so fast that I don't realize I have torn my pants. Everything is fine. El Negro has tossed himself to the ground, and grips the ball tightly to his chest. The play is repeated several times, and each time the forward leaves me in the dust, to the utter disgust of my teammates. El Negro flings every nasty word he can think of my way.

The match goes on and the bleachers slowly fill with fans. Other teams wait their turn to play. The thing gets more and more exciting. The audience begins to yell profanities, like at a real stadium. Tempers flare and the goalies shout directions from across the pitch. El Negro curses me out again.

"Move, goddamnit! Just fucking do something!"

El Guapo is our star player. He has made something like fifteen shots on goal, all without success. Soon, the ball comes my way, and that same forward who has embarrassed me so many times already, toys with me yet again. He fakes me out left and right, and the crowd is jeering. I feel an immense pressure in my chest and move without thinking. I fake him out to the left and kick the ball gently between his legs. The crowd yells out a long *Oooooolé!* and I kick the ball with all my strength. El Guapo launches it effortlessly toward one of ours, who headbutts it into the opposing goal. The thrill is incredible.

Next thing I know, I am hugging the scorer, and yelling profanities just like the rest of them. For a moment in time, the game becomes something important, and the field something welcoming.

The euphoria is short-lived, and the questions that had pestered me during the game hit harder, reminding me that I am supposed to be here to answer them. Why is this mass of young men playing soccer at four in the afternoon instead of working? Could it be that there's no work? Why can't they find jobs? Why do they need look-outs to be able to play? Why are we afraid when the calendar marks 18? Why is it likely that someone might come and shoot us? Why do we keep playing on a field where so many young men have already been killed?

My desperation to answer these questions is the thing that keeps me tied here.

The next team knocks us out in under five minutes. Immediately, another squad of seven players comes onto the field, cheering and hurling insults.

The bleachers are full, some four teams wait their turn, and a group of kids watch the matches intently.

As I head out, a steady flow of young men descend from the neighborhood and climb the bleachers.

# The Bait

EL NOCHE DOWNS his last gulp of Salva Cola then passes me the bottle, burping loudly. As is routine, the men fish for their cigarettes and we sit down to smoke and to tell stories.

A few days ago they tried to kill El Noche. It was Columbia Little Sycos of Barrio 18 from downtown. They failed. Their mistake was employing a tactic tired out among gangsters. *The bait.* This consists of sending someone to win your trust, then, banking on that, luring you out of the safe zone. Often with the promise of sex. Siren songs. Once at the spot you find a group of enemies there to eviscerate you. These deaths tend to be gruesome; the victim is tortured long before dying. This is precisely what was intended for El Noche.

Beside us stand Tombo, Destino, Hugo, and some others. Three cigarettes make their way through our hands. El Noche and Tombo share a knowing glance, then launch into an offensive of anecdotes they know will make their visitor—that is, me—blush.

"Hey man, do you let your girl lick your ass when you're fucking?"

"Nah dawg, I haven't tried it, but I do like to give it to them up the ass. Or finish in their mouth."

"Damn, dawg. Try it man, it feels crazy, besides it's not gay shit because she's a girl. I mean if a faggot licks your ass it's gay shit because he's a faggot but if a girl does it, it ain't, because . . . well, she's your girl."

Their eyes meet mine, searching for some response. They talk some more and look again at me, make a few explicit gestures, and look again for a response . . .

I entered this community through a religious congregation so it's unsurprising that the Guanacos Criminales Salvatrucha associate me with them. Besides, a little wooden crucifix hangs from my neck, by my mother's request, like Little Down and his amulets, my own form of protection. So the Guanacos think me a prude, and have fun trying to shock me.

"Damn man, so good to give it to them up the ass and pull their hair man, and damn do they scream, ha ha ha."

El Noche and the rest wait, between laughs, for me to say something. I think for a bit. They don't seem to be slowing down at all, so I join in. I tell a few anecdotes and El Noche and Tombo both seem satisfied. Or, at least, the jokes on me were no longer as funny.

Barrio 18's plan to kill El Noche consisted of sending a young woman to live in the neighborhood. Once there, her task was to seduce the gangster and get him somewhere his enemies could snatch him up without having to face the Guanacos. She succeeded. Well, at least in the first part. The bait seduced her victim, they had sex for several nights. Just as part two was imminent, El Noche discovered the ploy. The bait was a little too insistent, a little too intent on showing him *her house* on the other side of town. He knows this tactic, he's killed with it before. He took her by the hair and dragged her to a cliff. He took her by the hand and snapped her wrist. Then he asked her.

She resisted, maybe thinking if she denied everything she would have some chance of surviving. El Noche kicked her until he tired, dragging her by her broken wrist. She wouldn't talk, so he took her cell phone. There he found the answers he needed. Names and incriminating messages. Then, he says, the real beating began.

El Noche thought that it would be best to hang her. But he didn't. Or so he says. He says he let her go, battered and ailing, as a human message to the boys of Barrio 18.

We finish the cigarettes, and Destino gets up to tend to a plot of dirt where he plans to grow vegetables. Hugo starts kicking around a ball, and the two gangsters sit on the patio smoking and talking shop. Others arrive and join them. They, too, come with stories, some exaggerated, others backed up by scars.

The logic of this war reveals itself in fragments. With every story, with every action and reaction it seems to reveal its secret. Each day one can peer more deeply, and realize that for these young men there is honor in barbarity, bravery, and sacrifice, and that it is only *the cause*—their name for *war*—that makes life worth living. For this made-up cause, an army of young men kill each other, catching thousands in the crossfire.

It is impossible to know what really happened to the young woman who tried to trick El Noche. Maybe it's true that he let her get away with a few broken bones. Or maybe she is rotting several feet underground in one of the gang's clandestine graveyards. Maybe she'll come back, with friends, to avenge her suffering. If she's dead, surely others will do it for her.

# La Seca, Karla's Mirror

I T IS A little before 3 p.m. and the communal house is humming with the sound of kids. In the street, Moxy speeds around on my bike, nearly crashing into a parked car after eyeing a pair of women for too long. He turns the corner and speeds toward Columbia's territory. Moxy has been begging me for days to let him ride my bike. He put on a sweet face, and promised not to get into any trouble. I found excuse after excuse to avoid it. I said the steering was off, that it barely had gas, that, that . . . The stares I get traveling through 18's territory are already too close for comfort. I don't want them associating my bike with MS. That could get dangerous. Today, however, I am out of excuses and have no choice but to hand over my keys.

Moxy approaches the boundary of MS territory, demarcated by a gigantic amate tree. Any lower is hostile territory for Guanacos Criminales Salvatrucha. Moxy isn't quite that reckless, and quickly turns back, riding the bike through the air. Soon enough, he eyes the time and reluctantly parks my bike in front of the communal house. He hands me the keys and takes off running.

Inside the communal house things are better than last time. The kids are behaving better today, and we have extra help. Cristal is a neighborhood woman who offered to lend a hand. She is sixteen and knows how to work with kids. She's a teenage Claudia Schiffer, and the Guanacos Criminales Salvatrucha are crazy about her. In these communities, and at Cristal's age, gangsters are a sort of *perfect rebel*. The whole world talks about them, they are well dressed, respected, like the protagonists of their own movie. El Noche peeks his head in, hungrily eyes her up and down, and walks on. Cristal turns beet red and frantically fixes her hair.

At the entrance to the youth center is Karla, Hugo's sister. She speaks with La Seca,[22] one of the women who comes each month to ask Destino for money. Half of Karla's face is deformed by a gigantic red bruise that La Seca strokes gently.

"What happened to your face, Karla?" I ask when I see her, but it's her friend who answers:

"Nothing, she's fine."

"The man fucked me up!" Karla says irreverently, and La Seca croons:

"Look, being their girl is hard, it's a really hard life, you suffer a lot. You're still young, enjoy it while you still got him here, because when they are jailed up . . . that's hard. So far to go see him, getting up so damn early. And look, sometimes I go with four kids all the way to Ciudad Barrios, three hours to get there, and those long-ass lines . . ."

The four kids La Seca speaks of flutter around her, and Karla looks on in silence with the one eye she can still open.

It is a strange scene, as if La Seca were her reflection, a foreshadowing of sorts.

---

22  In English, The Dry One.

"It sucks dick, 'cause you can't even work or they'll say you're out chasing men. Damn, I just got a job downtown with a friend but he came out with this 'no the fuck you won't!' and, damn, at the end of the day you can't do shit," the girl says. She pauses, then looks around her, and continues: "I better go, because he said if I'm seen around these parts he'll fuck my shit up."

"It's because you're scared of him," says la Seca. "Look, me, when dude was beating on me, I fought him right back. I wasn't scared of him. Even when I was, I wouldn't show it."

Soon enough, like a bad joke, Little Down appears at the head of a group. He walks between the two women swiftly, nearly pushing them, and his group does the same. He seems to have taken the reins of this younger crew. They follow him everywhere. Among them are Moxy and Bernardo. Hugo still refuses to part with Destino, who for now is setting up an oven that a religious congregation has sent.

The two women, pale-faced, get up and leave. Karla walks down a hallway and La Seca marches down the hill, with her troupe of children in tow.

The gangsters enter the youth home and are met with kicks and insults from Hugo, who immediately gets a taste of his own medicine. Little Down gives him a swift kick to the ribs, sending him crying to Destino, who stares at Little Down with fiery eyes but says nothing. The recent arrivals are nervous, they chug their water bottles intently.

Bernardo is more animated than usual. He is no longer the timid young man he was a few months ago. He has a cell phone now, gifted to him by Little Down. He has killed his first man. It was the carpenter from a few days ago. The order came from the jail in Ciudad Barrios. The carpenter's crime was sleeping with the girl of one of the Guanacos Criminales Salvatrucha who sits in prison. He sent the order and the clica decided that Bernardo should be the one to kill him. This isn't privileged information, nor the product of an intense investigation. Everyone here knows it, several people watched a man take several gunshots to the face, but they have chosen to keep quiet. Again, Mara Salvatrucha imposes its iron law: see, hear, and shut up . . . or you're next.

As it begins to get dark, the first wails of the evangelicals can be heard. I say my goodbyes and take off. On the way down I can make out Cristal walking into an alley, escorted, ever more closely, under El Noche's watchful eye.

# The Fight the Bitch Lost

IN THE LAST neighborhood on the hill lived an old dog. One of those animals with no pedigree or anything. The dog was rat colored, with grayish-brownish fur, a curly tail, and a long face—as if it was specially designed to get into garbage bags. The dog watched over her house and her masters. When she wasn't eating from some garbage can or drinking from the gutters, she would bark defiantly, alerting her owners to the presence of a stranger.

When the PNC patrols would make their way up the hill, the gangsters would run toward the canyon and the dog would go crazy. She didn't like them running near her fortress, and the Guanacos didn't like getting bit when it happened. Once the danger had passed, they would kick the dog and throw rocks at her. The next time, she would bite harder.

The war between the dog and the gang lasted a while, until one day she was found dead on one of the cliffs, with a broomstick shoved down her throat. The gang won.

Today, things are tense. Everyone is on edge. Yesterday a car made its way up the hill, slowly, suspiciously. It stopped in front of the school. Two guns poked out and unloaded several bullets. Then they slunk back down the hill and weren't heard from again. Two men lay splayed out on the ground. They still wore their uniforms and backpacks, neither was even close to eighteen years old. Neither belonged to Mara Salvatrucha, at least not in any meaningful sense. The Guanacos are furious, they consider it an affront to their clica. The nerve, to go out and kill in their territory.

Everyone is fearful. Even the children in my tutoring session are tense. It's impossible to control them. It's as though they are possessed by some destructive force. They attack each other, cry, and yell, and it's impossible to convince them that a soccer ball can be enjoyed by several people at a time. Cristal explains that most of these kids, including her, knew the two who were murdered. Some even had to throw themselves to the ground or hide under cars when the hail of bullets fell.

Several gangsters stand at the entrance to the youth center. El Maniaco and Little Down, but also the new recruits. One of them is named Charlie, he's eighteen and has been deported from South America, a real rarity in these parts. He lived here growing up and has returned to find his childhood friends are now gangsters. He saw no recourse but to join MS as well. The other is a kid like Hugo, twelve or so, who looks at Little Down with profound reverence.

The youth center ever so slowly becomes a bakery, and Destino turns into something of a mentor for the kids. He spends the day working the oven and studying bread recipes. Moment by moment, this gangster loses his power. He does so willfully, subtly. But he still holds onto a bit, just enough to not get pushed around by others—and to stay safe himself. The clica respects him in their own way. Hugo sticks nearby. He knows Destino is his only shield. Otherwise, he would have to join the squadron of nervous hopefuls who follow

Little Down. Going back to normal life alongside his mother is no longer an option for Hugo. He is in too deep.

Destino has been working all afternoon on this dough. As I arrive, he takes off his baker's hat, offers me a plastic chair, and sits down in another.

"Ey! Let's have a soda," he says while putting a cup in my hands and calling Hugo:

"Dawg, there's the Salva Cola truck, go get a two-liter bottle. Tell those vatos I said so."

The boy takes off running and returns two minutes later with a plump bottle he shows us proudly. He screws the top off and chugs it down only to let loose a burp that echoes throughout the room.

"Hey, little bastard. Give some to Juan first, don't be rude," says Destino, and the boy pours me a thick stream of soda, which at this hour is like drinking manna.

# El Loco, A Game of Chess, and Little Down's Spots

S EVERAL YEARS AGO in the last neighborhood on the hill, on any old day, Little Down strolled with his black shirt down to his wrists, his amulets dangling from his neck, and a gun at his waist. From a balcony, a man peered out. The one that people say was made crazy by a witch. The man started yelling at the gangster, told him to go back to Lucifer and the Sihuanaba.[23] Little Down reached for his revolver without hesitation, closed an eye, and landed a bullet within centimeters of his head. The old man took off howling.

"See, he's not as crazy as they say," reflected the gangster on his experiment, and put the gun away.

Today, the heat is excessive. The sun makes everything bright and we sweat with the smallest of movements. Far away, on one of the neighboring hills, we can make out a fire. It slowly burns up the dry hill and its flames threaten to spread.

---

23  In Central American folklore, a shape-changing spirit that lures unfaithful men and drives them to madness.

The communal house bears a sign: *No tutoring today.* That, and no more. It is Gustavo's handwriting. Some kids show up, read the sign, wait around a few minutes, then run off in any direction. It never ceases to amaze me how kids manage to disappear into the neighborhood. Within a few moments, there are no signs of them. Occasionally you can make out their laughter down by the soccer field, if you make out any sign of them at all.

Before the house stands Jazmín with her juice. She is glum. She greets me then drops her eyes to the ground. It is clear she has been crying and it looks like she will resume at any minute. She tells me that the clica faces more trouble.

Yesterday, another police raid made its way through the area. They were silent, and undetected, taking Guanacos Criminales Salvatrucha entirely by surprise. The gangsters know their territory well, and managed to run for the hills or hide in the alleyways. However, El Noche did not manage to escape, and after a long public beating, they ripped off his shirt, threw him into a pickup truck, and took him down the hill. He won't be out for some time. He told me days ago he had a warrant out for parole violations.

Jazmín doesn't hide her distress. The other women in the community had murmured about an old relationship between her and El Noche, some years after the murder of her husband, Hugo's father.

"That is why I tell Hugo, 'Look, just look what happens!' Bunch of dumbasses, getting into trouble, watch them complain later. Now he is gonna be trapped in there god knows how many years," Jazmín says, more to herself than me.

The police are the third element in this war, a shared enemy. The police force the gangs to operate in semi-clandestine ways, and complicate their plans. Destino is convinced Barrio 18 and the cops around here have an alliance. I don't know how much of that is true, but what is certain is that of ten PNC officers, at least eight of them were here yesterday.

Inside the youth center, Little Down paces shirtless around his disciples. As he sees me walk in, he lifts his forearm and proudly shows off his new tattoo. It is an M and an S in black ink. The two letters cover his whole outer forearm. The tattoo is fresh; the ink still looks angry, and the S still bleeds. The other young men snap pictures on their cell phones and he admires it before a small mirror. He is happy, filled with some strange euphoria.

"I just got these done. They're for a killing, ha ha ha," says Little Down, almost possessed.

It seems he is in the mood to tell me about his crime; he follows me around as I leave my things in the room, and he tries to give me the details of his feat. But I don't feel like listening. His disciples have told me that he swears he's gotten a tattoo for each member of Barrio 18 he has killed, not counting civilians, a common practice among gangsters. This tattoo marks number five.

Suddenly, Destino appears. He has been listening from the other room, where he has prepared a formidable pineapple pastry. He sets it on the table and takes off his shirt, while looking proudly at Little Down and his small troop of kids. It is hard to find a spot on Destino not covered in ink. Little Down laughs dismissively and takes his troop out to the patio.

On the patio are eight gangsters. They are euphoric, spirits are high. It seems that Little Down's feat has obscured El Noche's capture. Among them is El Guapo, the gangster who took me to play soccer a month ago. He listens attentively to another gangster's story of how, in a village in Soyapango, his clica killed a Barrio 18 member with several blows to the head with a rock. Another common practice among gangsters.

They all laugh and cheer, then flash the gang sign. They look like kids celebrating getting away with mischief. Others have more stories to tell, each more grotesque than the last. The scenes are always in communities named after saints, the acts are always barbaric, and I am left feeling nauseous.

Soon, my salvation arrives. El Guapo places a chess set on the table and invites me to play.

"Ey! Juan, wanna play Ladies?"[24]

I tell him the game is called chess, "the game that makes you smarter."

His ears perk up when I mention it's a game of war and strategy.

"So, like, these vatos can only move forward. Fuck ass useless," says Guapo as I explain the pawns.

He continues: "Oh, so to fuck the king up you gotta get his girl first?"

"No, you never get the king, you just get him into checkmate, that means wherever he moves there's a piece waiting for him," I tell him, and he reflects on that for some time.

"OK, so the girl can move anywhere she wants and eat anyone she wants?"

"Yeah, Guapo. Except she can't move in an L shape, like the horse."

"Fuck! She's good."

Once he gets the hang of it and play a few rounds, El Guapo asserts:

---

24  Slang for chess in El Salvador.

*"This game is crazy."*

It is getting dark, and more gangsters arrive. I don't know most of them. El Guapo explains that they are from neighboring clicas. Allies of Guanacos Criminales Salvatrucha. I grab my things and leave the gangsters to their meeting, smoking weed and playing chess.

Little Down is still ever the hero and those who arrive hug him. I worry how Columbia Little Sycos will respond to his triumph.

As I take off, a gust of wind passes through and it is as if all the leaves on the trees try to catch it. The dust goes flying, forcing everyone to close their eyes. It feels like a deep breath, but it doesn't last long. A moment later the heat is back, suffocating us again.

# The Informant

IN FRONT OF ME stands a man with a cigar between his fingers. He sips a Coca-Cola. He is The Informant. That's how he has asked me to refer to him. Nothing more, not his age or description, nothing. In gang territory, that's how informants talk. He has been particularly bold, allowing me to record the conversation. But he cups his hands over the mic each time he mentions a name or date and devours my pack of cigarettes.

I met him only a few weeks ago, but he's been watching me closely since I joined the community. On several occasions I saw his eyes follow me, as if he wanted to say something but could not. Other times, while I wandered through the neighborhood, he followed me from afar. At first I thought he was part of Guanacos Criminales Salvatrucha, and that he was instructed to spy on me. As time passed I stopped caring much, until one day after hearing me chat with some gangsters, he approached me.

"Look, don't ask them so many questions. They're wary, you don't want them to think that you're with the cops. Just let them talk, they'll tell you plenty, but don't push it," he said, with a paternal tone.

From then on, each time we come across each other we speak for a bit, he asks how my research is going, cautions me again, and tells me a bit of his own story. It is a fascinating tale, but for his safety and mine it will never show up in any books. At least not in mine.

At the youth center, Destino is finishing up with the oven and Little Down meets with his troop of kids. They are planning a new strike. From what I hear, the plan is simple: send a woman to seduce the victim, sleep with him a couple of times, and deliver him into the hands of MS. Everyone throws in ideas. Little Down moderates. I jump on my bike and go in search of The Informant. Guanacos Criminales Salvatrucha are fully absorbed with their new operation.

The Informant tells me that there are several ways of killing, but that they all follow the same basic schema and have the same fundamental aim: a show of utmost brutality, to command respect and compliance. In this sense, the victim's death is a mere means to an end.

The first step is identifying the victim. For that, they employ a complex system that could well be called *espionage*. On occasion they send out kids with cell phones to take pictures of their enemies. Other times it is merchants, the ones who balance their baskets on their heads. The photos are printed and given to the man in charge of the operation. If it is his initiation, he has to prove his fearlessness. On occasion, they will be given old revolvers, with a mere three shots, or even knives and single shot weapons. Armed with these tools, the novice must complete the mission and live to tell the tale.

"Here's where you have to prove that you care about the gang. That you love the two letters. After that, when they see you got balls, you start to gain their respect. 'Cause look, if you kill an enemy who was well respected in his gang, you get that respect," The Informant tells me, a cigarette glowing between his lips.

The photos printed by the spies give the hitman a compass to find his victim. But there's still one fundamental problem: How do you approach the person who is set to die? It's complicated, considering that gang territory is governed by a strict security protocol. Every stranger who enters is corralled by a group of gangsters who strip them in search of tattoos or weapons. The hitman has to get creative to avoid arousing suspicion. Some dress as pastors and, bible in hand, pass through unnoticed. Others arrive as clowns, as Little Down described a while back. The makeup covers their tattoos. Even bakers are in some neighborhoods seen as a bad omen. On several occasions a merchant will park his bike in front of a target, honk his horn a certain number of times, as if offering his wares, and then continue on his journey. Minutes later a gangster will appear and finish the job. Sometimes the fanfare is set aside, and they unload every bullet they can at the first enemy they see, like with the young men at school a month ago. Whatever the case, at the end of each mission you must make it clear who was responsible. This is usually done with a loud shout: *"MS owns this shit!"* for example. You don't want to leave anyone confused.

I ask The Informant a question that I can't get off my mind.

"How does it feel to kill?"

"Look, at first it's scary. Think, like . . . when you're fucking a girl and it's your first time, you're shaking. You're scared, but after that it gets easy. It's just the first time, maybe the second, then the third is easy. You don't think about it hurting him or anything, you just do it."

A few years ago, a pilot group of sorts was formed. They were clicas made up of children, who basically played at being gangsters. A cruel form of training, with no shortage of extortion and killing.

In this area there were two, Esquina Locos Salvatrucha and Tienda Locos Salvatrucha. With the passage of time, the kids came to be initiated and joined Guanacos Criminales Salvatrucha. Among them was Little Down.

Back in the day, retirement was a feasible option. Later, things got trickier. They began to extort deserters, charging far more than these young men could afford to pay. Their options were to rejoin the clica, flee, or be killed. Some leaders would tattoo the faces of would-be deserters with the two letters.

Back to The Informant. I ask him about the present situation. How will this war end? He tells me things are complicated. Several Barrio 18 clicas have allied to push MS out of the hills. He thinks the last Guanacos strike, Little Down's, will not go unavenged. He says I should be careful, that in wartime mere proximity is enough to make you an enemy. I finish the interview and turn off the recorder. We share a cigarette.

On a corner are a few members of Guanacos. They look like a small army.

On the way back, as I make my way down the hill, everything is still. Buildings shuttered and businesses closed. The only light comes from my bike, and it goes out with every bump.

# Gangs, Champagne, and Pictures

IT IS AROUND 9 P.M. at a photo exhibition inside San Salvador's National Museum of Anthropology.

A French photographer speaks into a microphone to a crowd of well-dressed men and women. Wine glasses adorn the tables. Waiters serve delicate pastries. People clap politely at the photographer's every word.

"You have to be crazy to come to these places and do this work," he says in French, and a beautiful interpreter translates. He receives hearty applause, then continues: "And crazier still to bring your son . . . but what can I say . . . I'm crazy."

The Frenchman looks to his right and pats his son, also exceptionally well dressed, on the back. The audience rewards him with another rush of applause.

"We expected to find hoodlums waiting with a knife between their teeth, but instead we found little birds fallen from their nests. Forgive the poetry . . . I've always been a poet, ha ha ha."

The audience laughs with him, even before the young woman can translate. Most of them speak French.

The man speaking is Klavdij Sluban, a famed French photographer who has come to El Salvador for a project on gangsters in prison. He visited the youth jails for a few days—in Izalco, where the young men of Barrio 18 are held, and in Tonacatepeque, where the MS-13 men reside. He gave them disposable cameras to capture their surroundings. He did so alongside his son and an entourage from the French Embassy.

When he finishes his speech, the wine starts to flow. Appetizers too. Both are devoured, but with that same performative politeness. At the end of the day, they differ little from the Guanacos encroaching on rice and chorizo on the patio.

Photographs line the walls. Tattooed bodies, men with lost expressions behind bars. Single file lines of handcuffed men, blue cages, tearstained eyes, graffiti.

Guests wander through the exhibition, whisper, smile, and greet each other. They look at the photos like children visiting a zoo.

"Look, they're artists," says one woman to another, staring at a photo of an MS mural.

"It's beautiful! If only we could steer that creativity . . ." says the other excitedly.

The mural they refer to is in the Tonacatepeque jail. It is in memory of a deceased homeboy, and reads: *RIP Scuby, forever with us*. Its creators pose at its side, hands still covered in paint, profound sadness in their eyes.

Other women pose with the framed pictures, to be photographed themselves. Some call over Sluban and his son to take photos with them. One of them is Aída Santos de Escobar, a judge who has won a certain fame and secured her place in government after being featured in Christian Poveda's *La Vida Loca*.[25] Some academics wander nearby, studying the phenomenon of gangs. I make out a pair of journalists and some security guards. It seems the cream of the crop has been invited. They speak over each other with enthusiasm while emptying their liquor glasses.

Two older men laugh heartily while saying something in French. Behind them, in a corner of the room, El Noche of Guanacos Criminales Salvatrucha eyes us furtively from inside a picture frame.

---

25  A 2008 documentary that follows members of Barrio 18. Poveda was shot and killed by members of the gang in 2009.

# Calazo's Last Trip

IT IS MIDYEAR and the rains have begun. The humidity makes it hard to breathe, and people sweat profusely. Vegetation begins to spread throughout the hills.

Going up the hill is a true feat. The street is muddy and uneven, and the dirt threatens to dislodge itself, sending those of us on the only road that comes here tumbling back down.

But it's another sort of storm that has Guanacos Criminales Salvatrucha worried. Little Down's stunt did not go unpunished. Columbia Little Sycos did not hold back. Last night they murdered Calazo, a friend and collaborator of the clica, well loved in the neighborhood. He was a bus driver. Last night, on his final trip of the day, two passengers got up and pointed their guns. One at him, another at the other passengers. A few feet ahead, gangsters lay in wait, armed to the teeth. Before putting two bullets in Calazo's head, one asked:

"You gonna pay the rent or what?"

Then he fired twice.

They stole Calazo's moneybox and all the passengers' cash. The men were forced to take their shirts off in a search for MS tattoos. Then they were all told to leave the bus. A gangster from Columbia

Little Sycos climbed in, poured gasoline over Calazo's dead body, tossed a match, and ran. Luckily, an MS ally was able to put out the fire before it could spread. On the bus rode a member of Guanacos Criminales Salvatrucha. He managed to hide his tattoos, and that is why he is still alive. It is he who tells us.

Between the bus drivers and the Guanacos clica exists a sort of alliance—some might call it extortion. It's simple: the drivers pay the clica, and this not only guarantees that no member of MS assaults them, it also guarantees that no one else, including Barrio 18, messes with them. As time passed, a certain friendship developed, and now the bus station features a gigantic MS mural. There, the gangsters gather to play cards with the drivers. They travel by bus when they need to go down the hill. The buses are, in short, Guanacos official transport.

It is a bad blow, not just for the clica but the whole community. Calazo had several young children. The community is indignant and demand that the funeral be held here, at the communal house, since his parents live in Soyapango, Barrio 18 territory.

Some inhabitants have left the hill, fleeing their homes in fear. Gustavo, the head of the youth center, is one of them. Tutoring has been shut down for good, and Destino is in charge of running the center, which is now little more than a bakery. Chaos and fear reign, and people speak of nothing but war.

From the hillsides, PNC patrols can be seen. Pickup trucks make their way up and down the neighborhood, and except for the graffiti, there is no sign of the gang.

Destino is in the youth center. He is baking bread like nothing's wrong, though it was he who called me last night to tell me of

Calazo's death. He sounded more indignant on the phone than in person.

Destino doesn't like to talk of war. He avoids the subject and leaves when it comes up. But now he seems more open. He speaks of an old pact that today has been broken. Guanacos have always scorned the Barrio 18 clicas, saw them as kiddie stuff. But they always had a tacit agreement. Territory below the giant amate tree belongs to Barrio 18, and anything above to Mara Salvatrucha. This includes bus routes. It has been this way for years. Conflicts have ended in death and brutality, but they have never extorted in enemy territory. These sorts of arrangements are called southern pacts, in reference to an old Chicano gang alliance in Southern California.[26] It's not clear if it was Barrio 18 or MS-13 who broke the pact, and it matters little now.

Destino tells me gangsters often resort to these pacts in times of strife: "My kids live with their grandma in a bitch neighborhood [Barrio 18]. Nearby, in Zacamíl neighborhood. I used to hesitate about going. Everyone knows who I am. The thing is, they started fucking around: 'We're gonna kill your grandma,' they'd tell Isaías, my eldest. A while ago, some fucker put out a cigarette on Isaías's arm. I coulda easily gone and fucked shit up. If I had that mentality I had before, I used to not give a shit, I woulda set things straight. But I'm not doing that anymore. So I talked to the gang higher-ups, the mafia, you know. I told them what was happening and they told

---

26  This Sureño alliance is still in force today in California and other parts of the US. The enormous and complex system operates under the umbrella of the Mexican Mafia.

some others. 'Look, Destino's kids are being bothered and we want it to stop.' And the problem stopped."

Police patrols are an empty spectacle. After swarming the neighborhood like a horde of ants they leave, and the gangsters emerge from hiding. They come from every direction, always more of them. Reinforcements have arrived from other clicas to back up Guanacos Criminales Salvatrucha.

Alicia arrives at the youth center. She is one of the most powerful women in the neighborhood, one of those women whose tongue is a lethal weapon. She can make a rumor spread through the hills in a single day and tear a person's reputation to shreds. When her stories aren't enough to destroy her enemies, she resorts to a more powerful weapon: MS-13. She tells them of people in Barrio 18 territory who have made fun of the gang. The gang tends to punish these people. She is feared in the neighborhood. Today, she has come to complain. She asks Destino if they are going to take Calazo's death standing.

"So, you guys are gonna wuss out? Damn, that's fucked. Everyone's asking if you're just gonna take it."

Calazo's friends have also pestered the gang, demanding the same safety they pay a steep fee for each month. It is not just the Guanacos who are in this war; the whole community is red with rage at Barrio 18, and they want them to pay. There is an air of vengeance on the hill.

In front of the communal house, though it's early, Jazmín is closing up her juice stand. She tells me, anticipating the violence, that she has sent Hugo to boarding school.

"Yeah, I sent him to Izalco, a school with a priest. He can't keep living here anymore. I don't know how we'll get by, but I was losing him," she says, almost shouting. Then she lowers her voice and says:

"He's at La Unión but I don't want anyone to know, because I'm scared that man [Little Down] will go take him out."[27]

Hugo would never have gone willingly. Jazmín had to trick him. She said she was taking him to the beach, that they would play in the sand and swim in the ocean. And so at 5 a.m., Hugo dragged his mother down the hill, anxious to reach the sun on the beach. Hours later, the boy realized where he was. He cried, yelled, and threatened to stop loving his mom, but Jazmín had decided.

"Look, I already lost Karla. After she left home . . . now she's snatched up. So I don't want to lose this kid."

It is true, Karla has been devoured by the beast. She lives with Little Down, and he, with the obsessive territorial logic of gangsters, has marked her forever. On her shoulder blade there is a tattoo in gothic script: *Little Down*.

---

27  Izalco is a municipality in the western part of El Salvador, where La Unión is one of the country's fourteen departments. It is the department furthest from San Salvador, bordering Honduras.

# The Guanacos Setback

DESTINO HAD A dream. He saw himself seated on a gigantic bus that wove through dark alleys. The other passengers didn't speak to him. They looked at him with disgust.

He asked the conductor where they were headed, but he couldn't speak. He just stared and kept driving. He felt like a steer going to slaughter. A woman looked at him and asked:

"Son, what gang are you from? Do the hand sign, which one?"

"This one, this one!" said Destino frantically, signing the MS salute.

The woman looked at him with pity.

"Son, everyone here is an 18. All of them."

He took off running and found himself surrounded by walls confirming the same: here, Barrio 18 rules. Suddenly, hundreds of gangsters descended. From everywhere. The roofs, the doors, the ground. Destino whimpered with fear and ran for it, but anywhere he went he was surrounded. When he awoke, it was 4 a.m. and he was alone.

The war grows more intense, and daily life has become a pressure cooker. Guanacos Criminales Salvatrucha did not let Calazo's death go unavenged. It is no longer just GCS in the fight. Other regional clicas have allied with them. The same goes for Barrio 18.

Yesterday around 2 p.m. in Zacamíl, Barrio 18 turf, several people crowded around a TV. They were watching a Spanish La Liga soccer match. Real Madrid was facing its archenemy, Barcelona. The TV was in an alleyway. Cable is expensive, unattainable for most, and the device drew youngsters like flies to a corpse. Before Messi could strike his first goal, two men got out of a car, walked stealthily toward the group, and unleashed a hellfire of bullets. Then they claimed their feat, and left.

After the attack, victims crawled through puddles of blood in the street. There were eleven total, among them two little girls and an eighty-year-old woman. On TV, Messi ran across the field as the bullets echoed throughout the neighborhood. The wounded are in the hospital. Surprisingly, none has died. However, one has bullets in his lungs, near his heart, and the doctors say he will be dead soon. He is from Barrio 18, his name is Carlos, and those who were shot up are his family members. Five other men are in critical condition, all from the gang.

In the last neighborhood on the hill, at the youth center, Destino has company. It's Isaías, his eldest son. He had him sent from Zacamíl several days ago. He thinks it is safer for the boy to be with his father, in one of the MS strongholds.

The clica protects Destino. He may have lost power after focusing on running the bakery and refusing to lead Guanacos Criminales Salvatrucha. However, he is well regarded. He shared a cell with the higher-ups and risked his life in the most brutal prison fights. Besides, he's still the storyteller. It is to the bakery that Little Down sends the young to listen to Mara history. It is Destino who tattoos them with his homemade gun. It may be that Guanacos Criminales Salvatrucha do not listen to him like they used to, but he is still revered. At the end of the day, they know he was one of the first men to wear the two letters on his body.

Little Down has ordered them to send a TV to the bakery to keep Isaías entertained. The boy spends his time with his father, watching him bake bread. If either of them wants to leave, they are escorted by one of the Guanacos. They know if anything happens to him, the escort will have to answer to several clicas for letting the legendary Destino die.

People in the community are nervous. The attempted massacre in Zacamíl dominates the news, and rumors fly. Omens of war. They say Barrio 18 has attacked other clicas near MS-13 in an unbridled attempt to gain control. They said they have sworn to *get those MS fuckers down off the hill.*

The police patrols, as ever, fail to catch anyone. They scribble notes at the scene of the crime and stroll around with their automatic weapons.

The gang wars pretend to be simple while hiding a wealth of complexity. If you watch closely, their logic becomes clearer. You attack, then wait for a response. That is how the game is played. Each time is worse. Each blow is answered.

# Little Down's Reign

THIS WEEK GUANACOS Criminales Salvatrucha are inaugurating a new leader. He has promised to elevate the clica's status, to make them feared and respected above all. It is rumored that things are changing, not just for gangsters, but for everyone around here. Little Down's reign has begun.

The Informant tells me that if it was difficult to leave the clica before, it is now impossible. No more concessions, and gangsters and aspirants alike will face new obligations. The gears of war are turning, and Guanacos need all hands on deck.

The Zacamíl attack seems to have been a sort of coronation. It was a way of informing the Barrio 18 clicas that things are changing. That the hill still belongs to Mara Salvatrucha. The Informant tells me that after the death of Calazo the bus driver, there was tension within the clica. He tells me that Dark, the gangster I met that first day alongside Destino, has been steering the clica after the latter's withdrawal. However, complaints started to spread, and Barrio 18's repeated incursions did not help. It was then that El Viento,[28] the

---

28  In English, The Wind.

senior head of the clica, decided to make his move and name Little Down as leader.

"I've never told you about Viento?" asks The Informant as if it were a given. "Oh god, then you don't know anything!"

He tells me that El Viento isn't just the leader of this clica, but several others too. He commands his army of gangsters from a prison cell. He crowns and dismisses as he likes, setting their path from afar.

He was one of the young men delirious with admiration for Destino when, years ago, he still patrolled, gun in hand, in search of Barrio 18 enemies. In fact, it was Destino himself who initiated El Viento. But the clica's story begins a few years before.

Mara Salvatrucha doesn't really have a founder. Academics speak of an ex-guerilla named El Flaco[29] of the Stoner clica in Los Angeles. They say he founded the gang in the 1970s. An interesting take, as the war didn't officially start in El Salvador until 1980. And the first groups who could without shame call themselves guerillas were born as late as 1975. It was more of a collective movement, a cultural process.

In El Salvador, too, there was no sole founder. It was hundreds of young men who were marked with the two letters, who saw in the desolate landscape of postwar El Salvador a suitable niche for what they had known their entire lives. Gangs.

Those who came back cloned the gangs they had belonged to in Los Angeles. In this way, Hollywood Locos Salvatrucha, Normandie Locos Salvatrucha, Coronados Locos Salvatrucha, and Leeward Locos Salvatrucha came to be. It wasn't until the mid-'90s

---

29  In English, The Thin One.

that some gangsters began to create newer ones, with reference to where they operated. From this process arose the Teclas Locos Salvatrucha of Saint Tecla, the Iberia Locos Salvatrucha from the Iberia neighborhood, the famed Sailors Locos Salvatrucha of Saint Miguel, and the Guanacos Locos Salvatrucha from Montreal Street.

Guanacos Locos Salvatrucha was founded by a young man called Sky. It is not clear if he was killed or if he returned to California. Some say he was deported, others say no, that he was never in the United States. This is how oral histories go in the Mara. Unclear. There is no truth, and it all depends on who's telling things. Whatever his story, Sky's legacy lives on among other men who live, probably much like he did, just a few blocks from here. Sky governed the clica for several years, positioning it as one of the largest in San Salvador. The Informant doesn't know exactly what happened to him. What is certain is that the clica was left without its key leader. A few months later, they got a note in his handwriting leaving the gang's leadership in the hands of Destino.

Destino made it grow and took control of the territory. He did so with bullets, and an ironclad refusal to find a truce with the other predators who inhabited the area. An older gang from the '80s, the Gallo, resided here. They were among the few who resisted the onslaught of the two colossal structures that are MS-13 and Barrio 18. But they weren't the Mara's only competitors. A group of men from several years earlier had dominated the drug trade on the hill and a greater part of the city. They clashed furiously with the Guanacos and sent several to their graves. Via an informant, the Guanacos found out about a plan: the traffickers planned to call Destino and other leaders to a meeting to establish a truce, where they would be slaughtered. The MS leaders showed up anyway, ready for a fight. Several gangsters died, but so did the traffickers, and since then, the hill is theirs without dispute.

When Destino was put in jail the clica passed to Dark, who wasn't up to the task. When Destino returned, his role was more of a wise elder than an active leader. The clica fell into the hands of the most violent hitman that has ever been seen on the hill: Little Down. A great deal has changed between the Sky years and Little Down's reign. However, the logic remains the same. A handful of young men playing at war.

In the last neighborhood on the hill, a bus gets ready to descend. Full of passengers, it waits. It waits for Bernardo and El Maniaco, who eventually jump on quickly. They sport long-sleeved dress shirts and shiny black shoes. No tattoos or earrings in sight. One sits in the back and the other by the driver. Due to complaints by motorists on this route after Barrio 18's assault, Little Down has assigned a few gangsters to ride along on each trip as protection. One final passenger manages to hop on and the bus takes off.

At the youth center I am greeted by Isaías, Destino's eldest son. Inside, his father and another gangster discuss something important while kneading dough. As I arrive their language shifts, and I can't make it out. It's like a dialect made up of words turned backwards with numbers interwoven standing in place of words.

Two young men of some fourteen years enter silently. Destino guides them to a corner. The young men are nervous, sweating profusely. They look at each other for reassurance. Destino speaks to them closely, patting them on the back. They have been sent by Little Down, perhaps to receive final instructions for some mission, perhaps for advice or some sort of blessing. Destino leaves them on the patio and returns inside, to his bread. He is distraught. A gangster at his side looks at him and smiles.

The two young men sit in silence. They look at the ground, breathing rapidly, then nod and stand up. One is trembling.

Before they leave, Destino yells without raising his eyes from the dough, in that same gangster's dialect:

*"Chatru, little homies. Chatru!"*[30]

Hugo has returned to the community and takes refuge in Little Down's house. Neither the locks nor the constant surveillance could hold back this bright young man. He learned the schedule—when the doors opened, when the guards passed out, and fled. It is said the teachers at his boarding school in Zacamíl would beat him if he didn't listen.

There, no one put up with his tricks or his insults. There, he was nobody. He tried to threaten them by invoking his friendship with Destino, or his sister's relationship with the feared Little Down, and said that, if they didn't stop bothering him, the full fury of Guanacos Criminales Salvatrucha would fall down upon them. No dice. Now Hugo has returned to the belly of the beast.

More gangsters enter the home. I don't know them, they are from neighboring clicas. They look for Destino and speak to him in that coded language. One of them comes up to me and flashes the Salvatrucha claw.

"What's up dawg, what's good?" he says.

I return the gesture clumsily, and he is red with indignation as he realizes I'm no gangster. He looks at me, fury in his eyes, and asks Destino for an explanation.

It is time for me to go.

I say goodbye to Destino, and he signals an apology with his expression. It is night, and it's cold on the hill.

---

30  Pig Latin for Trucha, short for Mara Salvatrucha.

# The Guanacos Fortress

IT IS NIGHTTIME, and calm reigns on the hillside. Some five minutes ago I passed a feeble checkpoint set up by police at the foot of the hill. Just a handful of scared officers who watch the cars come and go. They pace nervously.

A shadow passes me by. The street has been paved, and my bike no longer squeals over potholes every few feet. The night, however, makes the trip feel interminable. I feel something like relief when I see those first few MS murals on the walls.

On a corner is a small flashing light. An older woman slings pupusas on a hot grill, and a small crowd contemplates her wares. They are wary of anyone who would climb the hill at this time of night.

Up ahead, the motorcycle violently thuds on the ground, and the sound echoes throughout the hills. A large mound has been obscured by the new pavement. A few months ago I heard Destino inform Alicia, the woman with the serpent's tongue, that the gang had decided to add some bumps in the road to thwart any stealthy police raids. At the time, Alicia just nodded and steered the conversation.

I thought it was Destino talking up the clica's importance, but as my bike smacks across the pavement I realize I was wrong.

When I spoke to the Guanacos about coming up by night, they said it wouldn't be a problem. But now it all seems different. Nighttime changes everything.

Every so often you can make out young men, phone in hand, monitoring the neighborhood. They are Little Down's newest recruits. Some recognize me and flash me the gang salute. It's their first mission, and they fulfil it with a military conviction. With this many watchful eyes, it would be near impossible for Barrio 18 to cause any trouble up here. Little Down's reign is starting to be felt.

As for the others, the hill remains silent. Even the police are nowhere to be found—the station is locked up and looks abandoned.

Every so often my motorcycle headlight illuminates a group of women walking together. Their heads are covered with veils. I barely register them before they retreat to the shadows. Religious services have ended in all the churches around here, and the hill is eerily silent in the absence of the pastors' usual cries.

At the last neighborhood on the hill, there are a few signs of life. More lights, and the last few pupusas before closing. But something else, too. The gangsters, who hide during the daylight, walk freely and proudly in their finest regalia. The smell of marijuana floods the alleys. The vatos are like walking chimneys. With night as their cover, the Mara grows stronger.

I park in front of the youth center. A group of young men watch over the place. They are gangsters from other clicas. I have never seen them before, and they have never seen me. They are taken aback. Little Down is with them; he has gone outside to yell at someone over the phone. I greet him to no response but a furious diatribe directed into the phone. The gangsters stare at him, as if to ask about me, but they too get no answer. They keep their distance, like wary street cats.

They approach ever more closely, talking among themselves and on their phones without averting their eyes for a moment. I can smell their cologne and hear their conversations, though I can't make out a word. I realize that there are more than twenty gangsters approaching the youth center. One of them nods at me, I am not sure if in greeting or as a threat, but my heart hammers erratically.

Their stares are piercing, and just as the pack seems poised for action, I hear a familiar voice call out:

"Hey! Juan, what's up? Come on inside, what are you doing out there?" yells Destino, and my heart slowly stops pounding.

He looks nervous, and a woman is around his arm. She is not much older than sixteen, and holds the gangster tight. Destino's look is flinching, and I see the glare of war in his eyes. He stares at the young men defiantly. They return his gaze for a few seconds, then huddle back to their phones. Now, things are back to normal.

Destino wields his power skillfully. He gestures me inside.

"It's going to rain, why don't you bring your bike in so it doesn't get wet," he says, pointing toward a corner.

Once inside, I see the reasoning behind all the security. Other clicas are here, as is the cowboy who struck a deal with Guanacos Criminales Salvatrucha a few months back. They discuss nothing important, they're just here. The hill is an impenetrable fortress, and in the midst of war it's for the best. They know that Barrio 18 will soon avenge the Zacamíl killing.

El Danger, from a neighboring clica, gives me a cigarette and beckons me to join their poker game. Destino digs into the Chinese food I have bought for dinner, and the smell attracts others. In the room, too, is Dark, the ex-monarch dethroned by Little Down. He is more tattooed than when last I saw him, and it's obvious by the way the others treat him that he has lost his power.

As we play, we hear rustling on the ceiling, soft at first and then harder. A storm has come. I ask one of them about the guys outside, and he says:

"They can suck it."

The night is calm. The rain is rhythmic and soothing. We speak of war only when necessary. The Guanacos and the other clicas are relaxed. They tell me Barrio 18 doesn't dare go up the hill, and for now they don't plan to descend. They know an invasion would be suicide. They know, too, that the Zacamíl killing has put them ahead, and the ball is in their court. Echoing The Informant's words, they tell me that several Barrio 18 clicas have come together to force Guanacos Criminales Salvatrucha off the hill. That they too are united. Several neighboring clicas have come together and, I am told, inflicted lethal wounds to their enemies throughout the town.

It is dawn and the Chinese food is long gone. Dark has made a small fortune off his poker winnings. Cigarettes are handed out and the room fills with smoke. The clica is calm. They know they run the place and don't plan on being seen beyond the hill for some time.

# The Bus

FLAMES OF WAR engulf the hill. The feud has left a trail of charred bodies in its wake. It was a raging night.

The Columbia Little Sycos made their move. Their escalation was brutal. Last night they intercepted a bus, one of those protected by Guanacos Criminales Salvatrucha, with all of the passengers—residents of the hill—still on board. They took them to the Jardín neighborhood, in front of the school. Right near where Calazo was killed just a few months before. There they were drenched in gasoline and burned alive. The men circled the bus, waiting for people to die. Those who managed to escape through the windows were promptly shot. Eleven people have been reduced to ash. Three more agonize in the hospitals. Within weeks, seventeen people will have died.

At the same time, other Barrio 18 members attacked a second bus that was ascending the hill. As the driver approached, they shot and killed him in cold blood. Despite the hail of bullets, they failed to stop the bus, which raced with its cargo of dead and wounded to the hospital. There lay Hazel, a six-year-old girl. She took a bullet right between the eyes and was killed instantly. The bullet didn't destroy her skull, it exited neatly through the other side, leaving her slumped against the bloody seats as if she were napping. The lucky ones cling to life in hospital beds.

Columbia Little Sycos, blind with rage, have gone all in. The Zacamíl massacre was not the only strike. Yesterday the Guanacos launched an attack on 18's turf, in the Polanco neighborhood, on a plump and bug-eyed gangster known as Crayola. They littered his head and chest with bullets in front of his family, and then fled to the hill. That night, as Crayola's family wept at his wake, the Little Sycos leader El Carne[31] assembled his homies by Jardín park's battered swing sets to plot their revenge. It was there that they arranged for the attack on the buses. A dark, short-haired gangster known as Fox ran out in search of gasoline. From the battered swings of Jardín park in a downtrodden neighborhood of El Salvador, a group of young men descended with death on their minds.

The Columbia Little Sycos had heard that, aside from the Guanacos Criminales, two others had a role in the death of Crayola: Juan Martínez, the bus driver, and his helper, Juan Erazo. Both from Route 47. They are both dead now. They were the first to be killed, before the bus was engulfed in flames.

Today at dawn, a woman lies comatose in a hospital bed. She is young, in her thirties. Her arm is smashed to pieces and the rest of her body is charred. Her lungs are destroyed from breathing in the smoke. A tube snakes its way into her throat, and the family has braced itself for her death. Yet the woman clings to whatever semblance of life she has left, that which the flames could not take. The

---

31  In English, "The Meat."

doctors were about to amputate the remaining shreds of her arm. For now, they have decided to wait and see. There is an air of resignation, as if the flames will soon claim what they left behind.

Before she was a charred corpse, before becoming a statistic, this woman had a name. Her name was Carlota, she lived in a neighborhood on the hill and birthed two daughters. One is twelve, the other nine. She had a home and a life. On Sunday, she and her daughters took a bus home. Countless times she had made the trip with her little girls, each ride mundane and uneventful. Not twenty minutes into this journey, Fox, El Payasín, El Wuilita, and other members of Columbia Little Sycos arrived with death—gunshots and drums full of gasoline. Avenging the murder of their homeboy with flames.

The incidents are straightforward. Each deed betrays its author, and these, like actors in a play, leave the scene one by one. Yesterday I spoke with Alicia over the phone. She is hoarse, and it sounds like a constant stream of snot is running down her face. She tells me that the neighborhood is limp with terror. She tells me, between sighs, that one of the little girls, the one with the bullet between her eyes, was her niece. The rest have yet to be identified. They are so charred, the women can't be distinguished from the men. Or, at first glance, the people from the scorched seats and upholstery.

The firefighters had to disentangle the living from the dead. The living were rushed to the Zacamíl hospital. The dead were placed in black bags.

I speak with Destino. He tells me the Guanacos are all accounted for, but civilians have died. He says he will explain more later, but for now all he can say is that things are hot. I don't think the choice of words is lost on him.

When Carlota felt the first flames engulf her, engulf her daughters, she beat the window with her arm, time and time again, with the insistence of a mother. With the insistence of someone who sees her daughters burning alive before her eyes. She beat it until she shattered her elbow . . . then beat it again, and again. When at last the glass began to give, her arm was in tatters. By the time the glass was cleared, her body was a sack of broken bones, engulfed in flames. Outside, her tormentors lay in wait to shoot those who managed to escape.

Today it is said that the Guanacos Criminales Salvatrucha have decreed a curfew.

*"None of you leave your house after 7. Blood will run!"*

A police helicopter circles the sky, and police patrols wander through the city. On the radio, a senior officer stresses that it is just a rumor, that there is nothing to fear. With a bus, passengers and all, reduced to flames, it is hard to believe him. The streets are empty. The police have captured eight members of Columbia Little Sycos. They are all young, and their handcuffed images are on the front pages of every newspaper in the country. They are dark, short, tattooed. They look so much like the Guanacos.

Despite the chaos, the police and the neighborhood know well that Barrio 18 is responsible. Another thing, too, is clear: MS-13's retaliation is not far off.

The war is all out. One gang makes a pact with the other. The pact consists of killing each other. Their status, and everything they know, depends on it.

After every blow, another follows, and like chess, each moving piece implies a play in response.

Little Down went too far with the killing of Crayola and the Zacamíl massacre. He also injured the families of other gangsters. He plunged the neighborhood into terror and indignation. So began the monarch's reign. Nearly two months after the massacre, and a mere day after Crayola's death, Barrio 18 has gotten payback, and in doing so has brought on an escalation of violence and barbarity. For now, all that's left to do is wait for the inevitable onslaught of Little Down and an army of young men from the Montreal hill.

Before the flames could overtake her, Carlota managed to fling her youngest daughter through the gap in the glass she had made by breaking her arms. Carlota's daughter was launched onto the street.

Outside, the men kept shooting.

Carlota faced a choice: bullets or flames.

I don't know if by then her eyes had burnt up, or if the flames had robbed her of reason. I don't know if Carlota could still see when the glass destroyed her daughter's face. The woman fell unconscious, and so she remains. She may never know if her sacrifice bore fruit, if her daughters—there were two—survived, if the result of so, so much pain was life or death.

The girls are alive. Alejandra, the youngest, took a bullet to the leg. She lost bits of flesh and skin that her body will soon regenerate. The eldest, Marlén, had shotgun splinters in her face. But the killers failed. They didn't kill her. They couldn't even do significant damage. The flames did their thing. But they, too, failed. They burnt the girls' skin and singed their hair. But the girls are young, and skin and hair grow back. This sacrifice was not in vain. Carlota, though she may never know it, danced with death and won life for others.

# An Eye for An Eye

GRADUALLY, MEJICANOS RETURNS to a tense sort of normalcy. People slowly fill the streets, meek at any provocation. The buses continue on their normal routes and the market is open, as usual, as if nearly a week ago seventeen people had not burned alive.

As for the police spectacle, only a small checkpoint remains. It is a few traffic cones lined up, as if to divide the street in two, and a pair of agents watch the cars drive by. Other bystanders investigate the site, still smoking, where the bus was set ablaze.

"Look, man, I'm going to be real with you. Things are gonna get real."

The Informant tells this to me in a small café some ways from the hill, like a preamble before he launches into an avalanche of stories. This time, there will be no recording. He says that people forget, but recordings do not. He is melancholy. On occasion a rage is seen in his eyes, the same one that animated him when he was with Guanacos Criminales Salvatrucha.

He tells me the clica is in dire straits. On the day of the massacre, the police captured Little Down and El Maniaco. It looks like both will be charged for several murders. If they're found guilty, they'll pay thirty years for each victim.

Little Down's reign is suspended for now. His glory days may be over. If the prosecutors do their due dilligence, no longer will he wander the streets, amulets up and down his neck, the very harbinger of death. According to The Informant, the cops got him that night in a surprise raid. A swarm of cops surrounded his house. They didn't dare beat down the door. They ordered the men to leave with their hands on their heads. Little Down responded with a hail of bullets. Guanacos Criminales' ex-hitman was not going down without a fight. The whole neighborhood thundered with gunfire. Little Down, with a tantrum of lead, managed to hold off the police. He took off, gun in hand, alongside El Maniaco. But the hive of police was unyielding. Even when surrounded, the gangster fought, but in the end he was captured.

I remember Little Down sitting next to me recounting fragments of his life as a Mara Salvatrucha hitman, his years in the Mariona jail under the fearsome reign of Bruno,[32] his ever-tragic love affairs, his years on the lowest rungs of Mara Salvatrucha, his fatal encounters with Barrio 18. I remember his dark almond eyes, glittering with rage.

It is rumored that the clica is led again by Dark, but it's just that, a rumor. Nothing is certain at the moment. Little Down has left the clica for good. The king of the Guanacos has fallen, and the clica anxiously awaits a new leader.

The Columbia Little Sycos, for their part, take advantage of the crisis to make another move.

---

32 José Edgardo Bruno Ventura is one of the most recognized capos in El Salvador's modern history. He was the leader of a prison gang known as La Raza (The Race) and was, perhaps, the most emblematic convict of the 1990s.

One night after the massacre, while cops and soldiers bustled through Mejicanos, up higher, in the last neighborhood on the hill, a squad of Barrio 18 prepared a third strike against the Guanacos. Two cars loaded with gangsters made their way up the only road leading to the community. They reached Dark's house. Silently, they descended in search of the temporary leader, and opened fire on his home, shooting anything that moved. What was left of the clica ran out to defend itself, and made the neighborhood ring out with bullets. It is said that for several minutes the clica defended itself rabidly, but lost against the onslaught. Not a single cop car made its way up the hill.

It is likely that Destino is right when he says there is a pact between the cops and the Columbia Little Sycos. One day after the massacre, on the outskirts of the neighborhood where it took place, the cops found the gun that killed Juan Martínez, the bus driver. It was a nine millimeter, the property of the police. It's not proof, but it's suspicious.

I ask The Informant how the Mara will respond to this invitation to barbarity. I ask if El Viento has given an order. He looks me in the eyes and says nothing.

He then tells me that Mara Salvatrucha's next move will be horrible and violent. Some have spoken of burning alive all the Jardín area merchants. An eye for an eye. It is common practice around these parts.

According to a PNC investigation, burned bodies have been found in the area for years, courtesy of the gang war. Others prefer a hellfire of bullets. They think the people in the area are all complicit with Barrio 18, and that they deserve the same fate as the people on the bus. Others, more modest in their vengeance, want to kill one of the gang leaders. It is not a complicated plan. They will send a boy with a camera phone, like a spy. Once he has gathered enough information on the subject, it will be sent to a squadron of men at the top of the hill. Another common practice around these parts.

I ask him if he thinks Guanacos Criminales Salvatrucha will survive the onslaught, if, now leaderless and disoriented, the clica will not succumb and abandon the hill for good. The Informant is thoughtful for a moment, and says no. Dryly, with certainty.

He tells me it's not the first time they have faced a crisis and launches into stories where El Viento, Destino, Calavera,[33] Casper, and Little Down save the day. He speaks of the war on Mara Gallo and their extermination. He speaks of Barrio 18's many attempts, and how they have been repelled for ten years running. He tells me this time will not be different. Mara Salvatrucha will prevail.

As for leaders, he says, it doesn't matter. There are more than enough candidates. The Informant eyes me slyly and asks:

"Have you heard of Garrita? El Viento and Sky found him in a park . . . that's what they told me."

According to legend, the two gangsters found a newborn. They saw, though crying and malnourished, something more than a child. They saw a way to continue their dynasty. They saw themselves in that child. So they decided to keep him, and raise him in the breast of the gang. The Mara would be the only family he would know, and he would learn to respect and love her from the beginning. The baby would be some sort of *chosen one*, and all of the area clicas would know and acknowledge him as a living extension of Guanacos' power.

---

33 In English, Skull.

They decided that the boy should spend time in each clica. The gangsters' women would see to his needs. As a sign of their pact, they tattooed his face with the Salvatrucha claw. It is probably one of those stories that grows more embellished with each whisper. The fact is, the kid exists, he sits in prison accused of homicide and sports the tattoo on his face. He is certainly a candidate for successor.

Calm has returned to the last neighborhood on the hill. The gangsters are hidden, and slowly people return to their lives. The first buses resume their travels. Very few are brave enough to drive them—or ride them.

Alicia is one of them. She gets on, empty pots in hand. It's a good sign, it means she has managed to sell her wares.

Jazmín still runs her juice stand in front of the communal home. She has given up on Hugo, and limits herself to cleaning his clothes and feeding him when he comes home. He is still in school, but the other kids fear him. *It is her fault for getting mixed up with gangsters,* say some. She is widely criticized, but Jazmín is unconcerned. She has another chance, one that grows in her daughter's womb. Karla is a few months from giving birth to Little Down's child. She has returned to her mother's house, and now they work the drinks stand together. They will raise the baby together, too.

The vagrant keeps howling in the streets, there is no ceasefire from the demons who afflict him daily.

Destino, meanwhile, continues making bread.

Gustavo hasn't shown himself around these parts. He abandoned his post for good.

The rest of Guanacos Criminales Salvatrucha are still children, eager to play at war again, awaiting an invitation, a new challenge from Barrio 18. It won't take long.

This war has ended, but a new one will start before long. One in which the soldiers look the same and the cycle of death continues.

It is evening, and a mantle of clouds clusters over the hill. The rain will come soon.

# Epilogue: Worse Days

December 2012

It has been over a year since I made my way up the hill, and there, and throughout the country, some things have changed.

Destino, after growing the bakery and recruiting other home-boys to his project, has been arrested again. The cops accuse him of leading MS-13 and roping kids into crime. They took him, nearly naked, from his home in a huge operation with dozens of cops and journalists at the ready. Isaías, his wife, and their infant remain at home. The accusations are unlikely; he worked full-time at the youth center for a Catholic congregation, well removed from the clica he founded. Now he will be thrust back in prison, probably Ciudad Barrios, the largest one allocated for his gang. He will be forced to navigate hierarchies and win back the respect that allowed him to survive for so many years within MS. It all depends on the court ruling that's yet to be scheduled.

Charlie, the young man who was deported from South America, sits in the Ciudad Barrios prison. He was convicted of killing one of the Columbia Little Sycos who participated in the bus burning. Moxy, the young man who asked to ride my bike, serves there too, charged with double homicide. He shot two laborers working construction in the neighborhood, supposedly because they lived in a place governed by Barrio 18.

In El Salvador the gangs have grown, restructured, and have somehow bent the government to their will. In exchange for cooling off on the homicides, they have secured lax penalties, and the transfer of their leaders to lower security jails. The pact has worked for now. From fourteen homicides a day, we now have an average of five. The authorities boast of having achieved the impossible: reaching a peace agreement between the two gangs. However, if you ask the people, you will hear rumors. It is said the pact will break, and what is next will be far more complicated and brutal. It is said that both gangs have taken advantage of this time to restructure and reorganize. Gangsters who expressed misgivings were promptly killed, like El Mafioso[34] and Droopy, murdered in the Margaritas neighborhood by their own gang. Several others have fled. Meanwhile, the scale of MS-13 has grown such that the US Department of the Treasury included it, in October of 2012, on its list of transnational criminal organizations that represent a threat to national security.

The Salvadoran minister of justice and his higher-ups pat each other on the back. Meanwhile, in the streets, the poor live anxiously. They sense worse days to come.

## June 2013

Edgar Giovanni Morales, alias Destino, was assassinated on March 6, 2013 by Barrio 18 hitmen on the skirts of Montreal hill. His death shattered the already fragile ceasefire and infuriated MS-13

---

34  In English, The Mobster.

homeboys at a national level. It is said that Destino was mounting his bike when a young man, dark and with slanted eyes, approached him gun in hand. They fought for several minutes, until the hitman lodged a bullet in Destino's head. He was left sprawled on the pavement, in a pool of his own blood.

Hours later, his homeboys set out on their bikes toward Barrio 18 territory. They killed several, including a police patrol. After a few weeks, a young man, dark and with slanted eyes, was found a few kilometers from the hill, wrapped in a sheet with obvious signs of torture and a bullet to the head.

Days after Destino's death, El Salvador's President Mauricio Funes declared the killing to be politically motivated, and those responsible for the ceasefire made no statement. They kept their phones off.

That same day, in the Ciudad Barrios prison, the fortress par excellence of MS-13, a raucous celebration took place. It was of the sort only possible after a ceasefire. A theater group performed in front of over two thousand homeboys. The gangsters, too, performed. In the midst of the festivities, a moment of silence was called for Destino. Thousands of tattooed heads bowed and silence reigned for a moment in that hell known as Ciudad Barrios. The gang's national leaders—El Diablito,[35] El Sirra, Snayder, El Trece,[36] among others—expressed their respects for their fallen comrade.

## June 2015

Óscar Sigarán, alias Little Down, was killed by police in a confrontation in February of 2015, when the ceasefire was irreparably broken.

---

35   In English, The Little Devil.

36   In English, The Thirteen.

After a shootout that left Óscar deeply wounded, a cop destroyed his cranium with the butt of an M16, leaving his brain exposed and killing him. In the same shootout, the cops murdered Trucha, Little Down's right-hand man.

## September 2018

It's evening, 7:30. Around when it all happened. We're at the edge of Jardín neighborhood, on Castro Morán street, where eight years ago the Columbia Little Sycos burned the bus with thirty-two people aboard. Alejandra, Carlota's daughter, is now eighteen and on the verge of completing high school. She's seated beside me, and I ask her how it feels to be back here. She ignores me for a moment, and stares on intently at the site where her life changed so much. There, her mother burned, as did her sister and her neighbors. There, she saw Los Columbia circle her unconscious mother and shoot her, multiple times, more times than she cared to think about. That night stole so much from her. But there was one thing it couldn't take from her. Sometimes, the will to live is just too strong.

Carlota survived.

The flames couldn't best her. Nor could the bullets. Nor the blow as she leapt out of the bus after saving her girls. Her will to live was stronger.

That day, the firefighters and cops left her for dead. Marlén, her eldest daughter, clung to her, and the cops yanked the child from what they thought its mother's corpse. They sat the girl in a patrol car alongside Alejandra, her younger sister, and three adults. Among them was María, another woman from the Montreal hill. Her body was charred, but she was still breathing. The car took off, and bit by bit the girls lost sight of their mother. Carlota was the last to be taken to the hospital. She spent at least an hour by a pile of charred corpses. They thought she was one of them. How wrong they were.

Carlota is seated by my side. I turn to her, and tell her if that night had been a game of poker between her and death, she'd be rich and death would be penniless. She laughs, and stares on.

Today, she tells me that when she arrived at the hospital she was unconscious. Her daughters were taken to a different hospital. Marlén, aged eleven, began to panic. She felt she'd left her mother behind. Let her down. Alejandra, aged nine, could barely comprehend the situation. At the time, her mind shielded her from trauma, distanced her from the events. Now, eight years later, the images are etched into her brain. With the passage of time, that merciful bit of distance eroded. She has much to process.

Alejandra says it started with a family outing. She says it was her fault. She whined and whined about going to the park that Sunday. Carlota had said no. They couldn't afford it. Carlota worked in the central market of San Salvador selling fruit and vegetables at a small stand. When things were slow, she'd sell afoot, bearing her wares on her shoulders. She'd clean up after other vendors, or run errands for a nearby restaurant in hopes of feeding her children. But that Sunday, someone gave her five dollars.

The girl insisted, it was nice out, Carlota had money, and she gave in. They went to Cuscatlán Park in central San Salvador. There, Alejandra played with her sister, they ran, bought a cheap plastic ball, and even managed to take an instant photo alongside her sister. They still have the photo. It too survived the flames, if somewhat charred and spattered with blood.

On the way back, they stopped to see their father. He has a bar downtown. They played for a bit with cousins, then went on their way. At a street corner, they waited for a bus. One passed by, they signalled to the driver, who ignored them. Another drove by. This one stopped. Juan Martínez, the driver, opened the doors and welcomed his passengers aboard.

Alejandra fell asleep on board. She always used to nap on bus rides. Not any more. It's one of so many things that changed for her that day. She heard yelling. A man insulted Juan Martínez. She smelled of gasoline. She heard the bullets that killed Juan, and took in her surroundings. A woman licked by flames put a child, who too was aflame, underneath a seat. Perhaps to save her from the gunshots that peppered the bus, without knowing the child was already condemned to death by flames. She remembered her mother breaking the glass, her mother grabbing her by the waist, her mother throwing her, she remembered the blow of the pavement, her sister's cries, the insults from the Columbia Little Sycos, the smoke in her lungs, the blood, the pain in her right leg. So much pain. She remembered looking back when her mother hit the ground. She fell face down, her neck twisted. She says she fell unconscious. Los Columbia surrounded her and shot her. They put five bullets in her body, not counting the shotgun pellets.

Carlota, when she awoke, thought she had lost her daughters. She cried. She cried so much, and so loudly, that they sedated her. The next day, she had a heart attack. She survived. She cheated death yet again, but death intended to put up a fight. Carlota suffered a second heart attack. They gave her up for dead. But she fought back. They transferred her to another hospital, Rosales Hospital. An infamous facility, where more than once the living have shared stretchers with the dead. An old, dirty hospital. That day, though the story had made national news, though the President himself had made statements and the eyes of the world rested on San Salvador, that day, there was no hospital bed for Carlota in Rosales Hospital. They had to wait until María, the woman who accompanied her daughters in the patrol car, had died, for her to be attended to. The pain was intolerable. Her body was charred and swollen. She got pins in her broken arm. She had bullets removed. However, a week later, no one had noticed her lungs had been damaged by smoke. No one there thought to give her a chest exam. Death is insistent when it sets its sights on someone. If it doesn't come by way of bullets or flames, it tries for medical malpractice. Her lungs lost forty percent of their capacity. She was hooked up to a breathing machine, and before long, with one last slight to death, she began breathing normally again. She left the doctors with breathing tubes in hand. She survived.

The doctors missed something else. Carlota had an M16 bullet lodged in her skull. A nurse found it while helping her bathe some weeks later. A doctor extracted it by hand, without anesthesia, and laughed:

"Look what you had in your head!"

We've returned from dinner, and Andrea, Carlota's youngest daughter, who was born three years after the flames, is winded from playing on slides in the restaurant's kids' area. As we approach Montreal hill, they tell me to be careful, that the men who now reside on the hill don't know me, and that the ones I met are little more than legends in the frenetic world of gangsters. I want to ask them something, but I don't. It's not my question to ask.

\*\*\*

It's June 27, 2018, and last week marks the eight-year anniversary of the tragedy. In a few months I'll meet with Carlota and Alejandra, but for now I'm in the San Francisco Gotera prison, in Eastern El Salvador. An ex-gangster arranges two plastic chairs as far as possible from the roar of the evangelical ceremony his associates partake in. He's young and thin, with bronzed skin. He reminds me of Destino. He sports a tattoo of his old clica across his face: On the right cheek, *Columbia*, at his chin, *Little*, and on the left cheek, *Sycos*. Now, he goes by his name, Gustavo. But before, he had different name, and a different life. In his clica, he was known as Fox. It was he who doused Carlota, her daughters, and twenty-nine others in gasoline over eight years ago, on a bus that made its way toward Montreal hill.

Gustavo remembers those June days well. The clica was on high alert, and the war with MS escalated more each day. However, that Saturday, June 19, one day before the attack, Gustavo decided to treat himself. He bought two cases of beer, got his hands on some drugs, and planned to spend a nice evening away from the stress of war. In Jardín neighborhood, where he lived, he came across his best friend. A man with slanted eyes that he'd embarked on an adventure with the past few years. Together, they'd launched a small drug business, together, they'd annihilated the competition, and together, they'd paid the price. A mere week ago they'd shared a jail cell. They were further linked still: Gustavo was dating the man's sister. They were like brothers. The gang called him Crayola.

"He was on a road with a bump in it. It's a nasty road, because if those fuckers follow you there you don't have an escape."

Crayola played soccer with two other gangsters and a group of kids. He was happy that day. Gustavo remembers him bathed in sweat, and happy.

"Dawg, let's go drink. Come on, man." Gustavo told his friend. But, ignoring his friend's worried tone, Crayola said he'd join in a bit, that he was playing. Gustavo insisted. Crayola promised to finish this match, then shower and head over.

Gustavo had had other friends die. When he was a kid, the Guanacos Criminales killed his best friend, Victor. The young boy had started to ride with Barrio 18, in the clica that Gustavo now sports on his face, Columbia Little Sycos. The Guanacos Criminales Salvatrucha killed Victor in front of him. They shot him, less than two feet away. Gustavo saw it all, it was a Guanaco from Montreal known as Marmota. Gustavo saw his friend's dying breath. When Los Columbia tried to pick up his corpse, an eye rolled out of his face to the ground. The next day, Gustavo joined the clica, and months later, Marmota died, shot on a bus. Marmota himself was close friends with another Guanaco known as The Blonde, who years later went on to change his name to something more imposing: Destino.

When academics declare that gang violence is cyclical, I suppose they refer to cases like these.

Some twenty minutes after leaving Crayola, give or take, Gustavo heard the bullets. He ran. He found his friend, still breathing.

"He was heaving, he made an awful noise from his chest."

Crayola died in his arms.

Another dead friend. Another friend killed by Guanacos Criminales. He cried. He yelled. He got the clica together, and called for weapons. He was ready to get those pieces of shit off that fucking mountain.

One option was to attack the Guanacos from the top of the hill, ascending by night and taking them by surprise. They decided against it. They were sad, but they weren't stupid. The hill was their turf.

The next day, the Columbia met up at a neighborhood park. They decided to attack what was within reach.

"The idea was, we'd kill the driver. Before that, I'd killed a driver, but I let the people off. The plan was to kill that piece of shit driver, and that was it."

Gustavo is lying. He tries to sell me on the idea that his plan was to kill, yes, but kill fewer people.

Gustavo was outed by his accomplices. They were captured that same week, and several of them talked. I had access to the police report. But Gustavo doesn't know this. He wants to minimize things. He doesn't want this visiting anthropologist to see a monster. This is the first visit he's had in two years, since the government cut off all visits and communication for gangsters behind bars.

He says he was betrayed by his own gang. He said it was the neighboring clicas, hailing from neighborhoods historically ruled over by Barrio 18. He says they wanted to burn him alive on the bus. Gustavo blames one of the neighborhood leaders, Xochil, or Rosado. He's a gangster who sits behind bars at the Zacatecoluca maximum security prison, better known in this world as Zacatraz. Gustavo says a great deal about that day. At times he takes the blame, but he's quick to blame others as well.

Gustavo fled. He was the most wanted gangster after his clica snitched. The cops hunted him for three years before finding him in July of 2013, in a routine raid in gang territory. The cops found a gun in the house, and so he was taken in. He tried to give them a fake name, but his fingerprints quickly gave him away.

He was sentenced to 466 years. He'll die in prison. He was moved to one of the Barrio 18 gangs. The gang leaders were furious. That fiasco wasn't on their orders. It didn't help the gang in any way. It only made more problems for them. They decided to kill him.

Another ex-gangster recounts that Gustavo entered the prison silently. He spoke to no one, and nobody spoke to him. The gangsters assigned to extract their revenge relished the work of death. They meandered, showing Gustavo their knives. People called them sharks. They loved the thrill of the chase.

"The sharks wouldn't leave him alone. They followed him everywhere, knives at the ready," the ex-gangster told me.

Gustavo had earned a life sentence from the government, and a death sentence from the gang. However, a year ago, the Salvadoran gangs had reached an agreement with the government. In short, the gangsters ease up on the killings, and they get better prison conditions. A prison death would throw that out the window. The sharks would have to wait.

Then, a massive transfer to Gotera Prison, in Eastern El Salvador. There, some gangsters joined an evangelical church, and their sector converted. It quickly spread, and by 2018, the entire prison had converted. They renounced gang life and now answer instead to pastors. It was here that I met Gustavo. I'd come with other aims, but once there, the pastors made me an offer that, much like at the youth center, I couldn't refuse.

"Want to meet the guy who burned down the bus in Mejicanos?"

We shook hands, and Gustavo grabbed two plastic chairs. At the end of our talk, Gustavo asked for a favor. A question for his victims that June on Montreal hill. He told me it was important.

\*\*\*

It's late. Carlota and Alejandra are anxious. They don't like being out at night on the streets of Mejicanos. Before our conversation comes to a close I tell them that I was at a prison. They stare at me solemnly. I tell them I was at a prison for ex-gangsters at San Francisco Gotera. They look at each other, their panic visible. I tell them I spoke with Fox, and they know exactly who I'm talking about. I tell them he has a message for them, and a question.

"I can't give you back your burned skin, or your loved ones who were taken that day. But I want to tell you I'm sorry, I'm really sorry. Do you think you can forgive me?"

Carlota bursts into tears. She says she's already forgiven him. That she doesn't hold a grudge. Alejandra is stone-faced. She stares intently, and says: "No. I'll never forgive him. I wish they were all dead."

We make our way up Montreal hill.